THE BOOK OF BEING BRILLIANT

THE LITTLE BOOK OF BEING BRILLIANT

Dr Andy Cope

WILEY

This edition first published 2019
© 2019 Andy Cope

Registered office
John Wiley & Sons Ltd, The Atrium, Southern Gate, Chichester, West Sussex, PO19 8SQ, United Kingdom

For details of our global editorial offices, for customer services and for information about how to apply
for permission to reuse the copyright material in this book please see our website at www.wiley.com.

Wiley publishes in a variety of print and electronic formats and by print-on-demand. Some material
included with standard print versions of this book may not be included in e-books or in print-on-demand.
If this book refers to media such as a CD or DVD that is not included in the version you purchased,
you may download this material at http://booksupport.wiley.com. For more information about Wiley
products, visit www.wiley.com.

Designations used by companies to distinguish their products are often claimed as trademarks. All brand
names and product names used in this book are trade names, service marks, trademarks or registered
trademarks of their respective owners. The publisher is not associated with any product or vendor
mentioned in this book.

Limit of Liability/Disclaimer of Warranty: While the publisher and author have used their best efforts
in preparing this book, they make no representations or warranties with respect to the accuracy
or completeness of the contents of this book and specifically disclaim any implied warranties of
merchantability or fitness for a particular purpose. It is sold on the understanding that the publisher is
not engaged in rendering professional services and neither the publisher nor the author shall be liable for
damages arising herefrom. If professional advice or other expert assistance is required, the services of a
competent professional should be sought.

Library of Congress Cataloging-in-Publication Data
Names: Cope, Andrew, author.
Title: The little book of being brilliant / Andy Cope.
Description: First Edition. | Hoboken : Capstone, 2019. |
Identifiers: LCCN 2018056464 (print) | LCCN 2018057535 (ebook) | ISBN 9780857087997 (Adobe PDF) |
    ISBN 9780857087904 (ePub) | ISBN 9780857087973 (paperback) | ISBN 9780857087997 (ePDF)
Subjects: LCSH: Self-actualization (Psychology) | Success—Psychological aspects. | Creative ability. |
    BISAC: SELF-HELP / General. | SELF-HELP / Personal Growth / Happiness. | SELF-HELP / Personal
    Growth / Success.
Classification: LCC BF637.S4 (ebook) | LCC BF637.S4 C663 2019 (print) | DDC 158.1—dc23
LC record available at https://lccn.loc.gov/2018056464

A catalogue record for this book is available from the British Library.

ISBN 978-0-857-08797-3 (paperback) ISBN 978-0-857-08799-7 (ePDF)
ISBN 978-0-857-08790-4 (epub)

10 9 8 7 6 5 4 3 2 1

Cover design: Wiley

Set in 10/14pt Frutiger LT Std by Aptara, New Delhi, India
Printed in Great Britain by Bell and Bain Ltd, Glasgow

CONTENTS

A Trilogy in Five Parts

Part 3
THE 3 Rs (RELATIONSHIPS, RELATIONSHIPS, AND RELATIONSHIPS)

Some solutions, happiness hacks, and easy wins to improve your work and home life.

Page 101

Part 4
WHAT NEXT FOR HOMO SAPIENS?

Mind-blowing stuff about consciousness and the nature of thought. Part 4 seeks to cement the learning from Parts 1 to 3 and embed new thinking until it's grooved in.

Personal development

Taking you to the very TOP

Page 167

Part 5
YOGI, BOO-BOO, AND THE HOMOS

Stretching the trilogy to a fifth part. *Really?* The missing link.

Copey
unfinished business

Page 215

Foreword

People often say they remember where they were when major things happen in life. For many it can often be a catastrophic incident in the world. They remember where they were on 11th September 2001, what they were doing when they heard the news about Princess Diana, or when Tony Blair told us we were at war once again.

Rightly or wrongly I've never really thought like this. For me it's what I was doing the first time I heard Bowie. Like, *really* heard Bowie, where it made me stop dead in my tracks. Or the first time I watched Christopher Reeve play Superman and it sent shivers down my spine. Or the first time I saw Ultimate Warrior on the telly, making his entrance to the wrestling ring and being transported to another world in my imagination.

These are the moments that stay with me. The moments I draw inspiration from when it's needed.

Never before in life has a book done this. And by 'this' I essentially mean 'changed my life'.

Movies and albums absolutely. Perhaps even the odd TV show. People definitely. But a book? No. I enjoyed reading but was never a reader.

That was until 2012.

I happened to find myself in a well-known high-street bookstore with my young son. I seem to remember *The Gruffalo* being the order of the day. As we headed for the checkout I was drawn to a book called *The Art of Being Brilliant*.

What a shit title for a book I thought. *Who even buys this pish?*

I felt compelled to have a flick through. Every page I stopped on smacked me in the face with truth and wit. The way it was written was just how I think. It was like someone had climbed into my brain and stolen all my thoughts, made sense of them, and put it in a fucking book. It was my book. Who's this arsehole that's written my fucking book?

Andy Fucking Cope.

Absolutely furious, I bought it.

And then I read it. And then I read it again. I read it twice in one sitting. It made me laugh, it made me cry (Jimmy's Diary), it made me think, it made me angry, it made me think some more, and, most importantly, it made me do. It gave me permission to do all the things I'd thought about but didn't know how. It brought clarity and focus to a very busy head. It gave me a sense of belief.

I loved it. I still do. And I love Andy Cope for writing it.

Fast forward a few years and our paths finally crossed. They say you should never meet your heroes as it's never what you hope it's going to be.

David Bowie. Christopher Reeve. Ultimate Warrior. Andy Cope.

Andy is one of my heroes. Unlike my other heroes he's very much alive. I met him, and he was everything I hoped he would be.

We talked. We ate soup. He asked me to write a book with him. I said yes. We wrote *SHINE*, the best self-help book ever written.

BOOM.

And now he's penned this one, the *second* best self-help book ever written! It's Andy's greatest hits, gathered together in one epic page-turner. No plot spoilers from me but it's got everything you *wouldn't* expect from a personal development book; goats, Munchkins, Bon Jovi, the paranormal Olympics, the word *erschlossenheit*, and an actual chapter called 'Yogi, Boo-Boo, and the Homos'. He even dares to pick a fight with Buddha and literally nobody ever does that, ever.

Laugh, cry, squirm, and learn. You'll remember where you were when you read *The Little Book of Being Brilliant*.

Enjoy!

Gavin Oattes
Trainer, keynote speaker, stand-up comic
and best-selling author

Thinking Allowed

olives

19th July, 9.48pm. Picture this. My wife and I are sitting on a patio in Majorca. Inland Majorca. Classy. Not Magaluf Majorca. The sun's set and we're winding down after a hard day of winding down.

I like to think of myself as a go-getter, someone who squeezes the maximum out of life. But I also like to be in bed by 9pm. Holidays are different. It's more like 10 or even 10.30. Lou's reading a trashy novel. I look up from my Kindle and ask, 'Tourette's. Why is it always negative? Why don't they blurt lovely stuff. "I love you!" "You're amazing!" "Gosh, look at that sunset" kind of thing?'

Lou reaches for an olive but doesn't break away from her book. 'Repressed thoughts', she replies as the olive goes in.

I'm impressed. She's guessing, obviously. But logic tells me she's right. Tourette's must be what Freud was rabbiting on about with his Id and Ego stuff. However, it's not her actual answer that spurs me on, rather her ability to have this thought while choosing an olive and without breaking away from her chapter. Multi-tasking at its best.

'Do you ever wonder about your thinking? You know, *think* about your thinking?'

She sighs and breaks away from the book. 'I'm aware of it now,' she huffs. 'When it gets interrupted. And at night. When it keeps me awake.'

I decided to prod. Gently. 'So, at 3am you're lying there thinking? You're thinking so much that it's keeping you awake. You're the one doing the thinking.'

'Yes. Obviously.'

'If you're the one doing the thinking, have you ever thought who's the one *noticing* that you're thinking?' Please note, this is the kind of conversation that you can only have after 25 years of marriage. It's not a first date question. At least, not if you're wanting a second.

Lou penetrates the Majorcan dusk with one of her Paddington stares. There are no words but just the merest shaking of her head which I'm taking to mean *WTF? You're disturbing me from my book, for this?*

'Or that nothing's real?' I dare to venture. 'It's all created in your mind. Literally everything. Your book. Even Majorca.'

She adds a sigh and long blink to her Paddington stare. She hits her book against the table so there's a loud thud which, to be fair, is a good way of making her point. I have to admit, her book does look real.

'Majorca's not real? That's ridiculous shit. It's an island. We're sitting on it. Whatever's in your head, write it down and we'll publish it when you're dead. I don't want people thinking you're a dick while you're alive.'

I resumed my Kindle chapter thinking she's probably right. The world's not ready for this.

At least not until Part 4.

Part 1

WELCOME TO THE PLEASURE DOME

It's an awakening. Hello. *Helloooooo!* WAKEY WAKEY! The best way to make your dreams come true is to wake up.

Life's for living, so let's crack on …

In true Sesame Street tradition, each section of the book is brought to you in association with a new word. Part 1 is sponsored by the word **Sólarfrí.** Icelandic / n. / saʊ.lɑ:fri: / soh-lah-free. A sun holiday, i.e. when workers are granted unexpected time off to enjoy a particularly sunny/warm day.

Enough Already!

Have you ever tried to write a book? For the uninitiated (and I appreciate this might just be me) it doesn't start with pen, paper, or laptop. It kicks off with cleaning my fridge out. Nine times. Then you spend some time alphabetizing your CD collection and sorting your spice rack. Then you open your laptop and some emails have pinged in. *Well they'll need answering, rude not to.* Then you'll have your usual webpages and social media accounts to check out. I'll generally bleach the toilet and then stick the kettle on because I can't write without coffee.

Back to my desk and a few more emails have popped in – *gosh I'm soooo popular* – and someone's retweeted a couple of my tweets. I have to return the compliment, obviously!

Then I decide to change the CD system. It's been niggling me. I'm overloaded with Ts, because foolishly I've put The Clash, The Ramones, The Carpenters, The Who, and all the other

'The' bands under 'T'.
Schoolboy error. With
'The Clash' now safely
categorized alongside
Chopin, I sit down at my
laptop, crack my fingers
and knuckles, take a deep
breath, and decide it's time
for a sandwich.

> We all know Jesus was
> a carpenter but he
> never actually sang on
> any of their records.
>
> *Mark Walker*

And so to business.

Welcome to book 11. Yes, eleven! I'm
counting them on my toes.

Double figures feels like an anniversary.
A time to look back and reflect.

You might be such a loyal follower that
you've read and absorbed all eleven.
In which case, I salute you. A warrior

of personal development. You've read them on the beaches.
You've read them in the hills. You've never surrendered. You've
been with me through the mud and bullets.

Or you might have casually picked this book up at the airport
and are wondering who the heck I am?

I've written this book for both sets of readers. After 11 albums,
David Bowie was allowed a Greatest Hits compilation. Ditto
Fleetwood Mac, Abba, and Bon Jovi. I think Kajagoogoo had a
greatest hits album too?

Anything Kajagoogoo can do I can do too.

Isn't it about time I stopped being too shy shy and compiled the last 10 years of writing into one simple tome? Whether you deem it to be a timeless classic or pop fluff, I've delegated that judgement to you.

With that burden lifted from my shoulders I'm free to crack on with track 1 which is, I believe, something of a wedding playlist containing, as it does, something old, new, and borrowed.

But first, something blue.

Check the book charts and you'll notice a pattern to the current crop of bestsellers. As a result, I toyed with calling book 11 'The little book of being TOTALLY FUCKING brilliant'.

Thankfully, I'm not that desperate for a number 1 hit. Yes, some naughty words might creep in, but not emblazoned on the cover where the kids can see them. I'm not a monster.

Here's a beautiful non-naughty new word for you: Sonder. You know that craziness in your head, the whirring of thoughts and insecurities? Sonder is the realization that each random passer-by is living a life as vivid and complex as your own – populated with their own ambitions, dreams, routines, worries, and inherited craziness. Sonder hints that the inner dialogue always veers towards the negative and it ain't half shouty.

But it's not just you! Sonder applies to the human race. Yes, everyone else is insecure too, even the ones who seem to have their shit totally together. They actually haven't! They're filled with self-doubt and the same negative shouty voice, so chill, we're all a little bit crazy and a whole lot insecure.

Sonder means you and I are alike. It's easy to become addicted to the endless cycle of lack, an emptiness, a feeling that there should be something more. Your life feels like the second-hand jigsaw you bought from a car boot sale – you don't rejoice that there are 497 jigsaw pieces, you fret at the missing 3.

We're all gripped with a nagging feeling that something's missing. Your *je ne sais quoi*. Death is coming, life is relentless, what on earth are we to do?

Chaos is the new normal. I used to feel like one of those cartoony figures that's just run through a wall, leaving a massive Andy-shaped hole. I set out to fill the hole with wi-fi, money, midnight snacks, work, and general busyness. Rather than create gaps in my diary I was always looking to fill them because … well because that's what everyone else was doing.

Andy-shaped hole

For me, the starting point is a little darker. I was always told that death and taxes were inevitable and then I discovered that the uber rich have off-shore trusts in Panama.

So it's just death then.

> Conversation in *Hitchhiker's Guide to the Galaxy* between Arthur Dent and Marvin the Paranoid Android:
>
> **Arthur:** 'Marvin, any ideas?'
>
> **Marvin:** 'I have a million ideas. They all point to certain death.'

We're all familiar with 'presenteeism' at work, that feeling of turning up and going through the motions. But it's a much bigger concept than work. Presenteeism can apply to life. You're centre-stage, the leading player in your own life, but struggling to engage with the plot.

There's a creepy line of dialogue in the movie *The Sixth Sense* where the haunted young boy tells Bruce Willis, 'I see dead people.' I think I have a similar 'gift', except that the people aren't physically dead, they're those living a near-life experience, thousands of them going about their lives in a zombie-like trance of mediocrity. Technically, they are alive. There's a pulse. But not much else.

So, before I hit you with a barrage of philosophy and 'ologies', let me start where I always bloody well start, with Stephen Covey's 'begin with the end in mind'. If I'm talking to a room full of children and I announce that the average lifespan is 4000 weeks I'm treated as some sort of demi-God. There's a lot of jumping and cheering – 'Woo-hoo, thanks for telling us, Andy. That's like … forevs!'

The same fact shared with a corporate audience and I'm the anti-Christ, pelted with soft fruit. The childlike woo-hoo becomes an adult boo-hoo. Sometimes

> 'I'm normally not a praying man, but if you're up there, please save me Superman.'
>
> *Homer Simpson*

people will vocally disagree. 'That can't be right', they say, tapping some numbers into their smartphone, discovering not only that it's true but also sobering. *Gulp! 4000 weeks is not a very big number. And I've used a few!*

If your goal is perfect peace, I think you might have to wait until your 4000 weeks have been consumed. It's like a Premiership game – eventually someone will hold a board up with your number on – human being number 7,455,632,001 – *shit, that's me! The gaffer's decided I've had enough.* You trudge off the game of life to warm applause and someone takes your place, a fresher pair of legs.

You can enjoy your bath in perfect peace. Eternal soulful peace, hopefully.

11

But if you want a quieter mind and more fulfilling *earthly* existence, you've got your nose in the right book.

Sonder; the yearning, the inner agitation of 'is this it?', it's there for a reason. It's trying to lead you somewhere.

It boils down to this: if there's something missing in your life, it's most probably you.

Welcome home.

Begin with the End in Mind

In the interests of life being a short and precious gift, I thought I'd throw this one at you:

> *Richard's nickname was dig bick*
> *You that read wrong!*
> *You read that wrong too![1]*

Apologies if it caught you out. It means you're skimming the surface of this book, hoping to speed read your way to enlightenment. I understand your impatience. I don't want to twist the knife any more than I have to but there's a good chance you're skimming the surface of life too. You've become what human beings are – a race – a seething mass of seven billion runners competing in a 4000-week sprint.

---

[1] *Stolen mercilessly from* How to Have a Great Life *by Paul McGee.*

Modern life is hectic and full on. I recently had an exasperated delegate on one of my workshops who huffed and puffed that 'I haven't got time to be happy!'

> 'I went to a bookstore and asked the saleswoman, 'Where's the self-help section?' She said if she told me, it would defeat the purpose.'
>
> George Carlin

Happiness doesn't require time, it requires insight. It might require a refocusing away from your to-do list towards your to-be list, because 'who are you being while you're doing the things on your list' requires you to point the finger back at yourself and ask some searching questions. There's a degree of honesty involved too. Are you being full of optimism, happiness, hope, energy, positivity, enthusiasm, and vivacity? Or are you being like everyone else, who pretty much isn't?

Society is experiencing a massive 'wait problem'. The mantra, insidiously seeping into you from a very early age, is that Mondays are bad and Fridays are good. Oh, and Wednesdays aren't too bad because it's all downhill from there. Once that way of thinking is firmly lodged in your head, it's difficult to get it out again. You become that person. You slouch on Mondays and skip on Fridays. You're waiting for life's happy hour.

But here's where it gets really spooky because nobody sat you down and taught you that Mondays are rubbish and Fridays awesome.

Who taught you this?

Monday Tuesday Wednesday Thursday Friday

When I was four my dad never sat me down for a chat and said, 'Look here little Andy, there's some stuff you need to know about life, so I'm going to tell you straight.'

'What is it Dad?' I ask adoringly. In my eyes, age four, my dad is God.

'Well son, first of all you need to know that Mondays are bad. I mean really stinky. And Tuesdays aren't much better. Wednesdays pick up a bit but they're still a bit pants. Thursdays are a bit better then you can come alive on a Friday.' He swells his chest as he recalls that Friday feeling. 'Yes indeed. Fridays are good because Saturday comes next and let me tell you son, Saturday is the best day of the week by far. You can proper enjoy Saturdays.' He pauses, breathing in the intoxication of Saturday and then exhaling as he considers how he's going to explain Sunday to his 4-year-old. 'Sundays, well they're okay 'till about 4 o'clock and then you start to get depressed again because Monday comes next.'

I'm nodding, taking it all in. Dads never tell fibs.

'And son, you're gonna do that 4000 times and then you'll die.'

I don't know about you but that conversation never actually took place in my house. It didn't need to. The fact that my dad slouched out of the house on Monday and kangarooed in on Friday was clear enough.

That's how I learned. And me and thee are the same. Human beings have an in-built social satnav that has a magnetic gregarious pull towards other people. There are social rules that we need to abide by if we want to be part of a tribe, clan, team, or family. And this social magnetism pulls us into strict conformity.

In the olden days, being excluded from your tribe was effectively a death sentence and the new world equivalent, being unfriended on Twitter, hurts like hell too. Because being part of something social plays such an important part in your well-being you end up falling into line.

If you buck the trend by leaping into the office on a Monday with a hearty cry of 'Don't those weekends drag …' then the chances are, you won't have any friends, either on Facebook or anywhere else.

So, the majority of the population learn the behavioural ropes and go about their hectic lives, fitting in as best they can. As William Deresiewicz rightly points out, we become the world's most excellent sheep.[2]

So, unless you're incredibly enlightened, this is how life plays out. You have a vague idea of what you want; more money and recognition maybe? Less stress perhaps? Or a nice holiday where you can relax and recharge your batteries. You want to be purged of 'minor glumness', that feeling that sits in the pit of your stomach when the alarm goes off at stupid o'clock on a work day. It's akin to Phyllis Diller's 'morning sickness' – she wasn't pregnant, just sick of mornings!

Sound familiar?

Baa-aa.

---

[2] W. Deresiewicz (2014) Excellent Sheep: The miseducation of the American elite and the way to a meaningful life. New York: Simon & Schuster Children's Publishing.

The Shortest Book in the World

> 'We live in an uncaring society. I was in the park the other day watching an old man feed the birds, and after a while I thought to myself: I wonder how long he's been dead?'
>
> *Milton Jones*

Muhammad Ali holds the world record for the shortest poem ever, a pithy two-worder that he made up on live TV, which goes like this;

Me. We.

I like it because it points towards human connection, introspection, 'outro-spection' – and because it rhymes, like poems bloody well should. But mostly I like it because it's short.

Imagining that you're pushed for time I was tempted to take a leaf from the pugilistic wordsmith and make this the shortest personal development book ever. If I was to take the money and run and we could be done in a couple of pages.

I'd have called it *The Cheat's Guide to Awesomeness* and the double-pager would be this:

Hello.

We hear a lot about fake news. Here's the real news which, to be fair, you'll be wishing was fake news. It comes in two dollops; bad, and then *reaaaaally* bad.

The bad news is that you're going to die.

The really upsetting bit is that so is everyone else.

I suspect that death itself isn't the problem. It might be a bit scary, all that 'not breathing', and as you're drawing your last breath there will be the worry of whether you've left the gas on and who will feed the cat.

But it's not death that's the source of our mortal teeth gnashing, rather the fear that we might not have lived quite the joyous and fun-filled life that we might have.

Four thousand earthly weeks of mediocrity is such a terrible waste of time!

Fact #1: the world isn't going to bend to accommodate your wishes. If your happiness is contingent on the arrival of the perfect political party, cloudless azure skies, the elimination of pot holes, and cheap trains that run on time, you'll die waiting.

Fact #2: the biggest obstacle to your awesomeness is yourself.

Now you know what the problem is, the even better news is that, with laser precision, you already have the answers. You already know how to improve your state of well-being. Don't believe me? Try this:

List three things you can do, starting today and doing them every day, that will seriously improve your life:

1.
2.
3.

Remember, I'm aiming to write the shortest personal development book in the world, a two-page wonder. You have identified the problem and come up with three easy-peasy solutions but we still haven't filled the two pages. So, as a filler, let's throw in the opposite question:

List three things you can *stop* doing, or do less of every day, that will seriously improve your life:

1.
2.
3.

Please *go* and do the things you said would help and stop doing the things that are harming your well-being.

Thank you for reading *The Cheat's Guide to Awesomeness*. Enjoy the rest of your fabulous life.

The end.

This glorious piss-take is frustrating as hell because you know it's true. Or half true, at least.

There's a difference between 'knowing' and 'doing', hence the rest of this book. You need knowledge. You need confidence to experiment. You need the motivation to change but most of all you need some hand-holding, coaxing, scaring perhaps? (hence the death stuff)

I spend a lot of time in organizations trying to fix people and teams who have had some vastly overcomplicated restructure or culture change initiative that hasn't worked. Getting rid of people is harsh enough but the modern game is to make it even more cruel by asking people to re-apply for their own jobs, like some kind of organizational musical chairs. The rules are simple enough: when the music stops, two of you will have had your desks cleared and there'll be nowhere for you to sit.

Smile now (through gritted teeth, obviously) as Black Lace's *Superman* blares out …

The music stops when you're mid 'macho-manning', there's a mad scramble for chairs, a couple of players leave the game, and the remaining ones have to graft harder to cover the players who are out.

The music cranks up again …

Enough!

Let's quit playing the same game as everyone else. It's about time you took charge of the music and danced to your own tune.

Lubed Up and Ready for Action

Solutions? They come later. First let's have a sneaky peek behind the curtains of modernity. If we can catch sight of the problems, we stand a better chance of finding a way forward.

Congratulations on your membership of the most exclusive club ever. In fact the first of its kind in human history, and you're a gold member. The elite. You are a member of the most in-debt, medicated, obese adults in the history of the human race.

The world has always been a dangerous place. The terror used to come from scarcity – not enough food, clean water, warmth, or medicine. The lack of pretty much everything meant that if you reached 40, you were living a charmed existence. We tend to forget that since Homo sapiens were invented we've been eking out an existence, surviving from day to day, season to season. A bad crop and the village is wiped out. Appendicitis meant curtains. A dodgy water supply meant dysentery and death by diarrhoea. That's a really shitty way to go.

The world is still dangerous, but the terror pendulum has swung from extreme lack to gratuitous excess. Too much food, drink, and medication. We're dying of ailments caused by excess. Obesity, type 2 diabetes, heart attacks, alcoholism, stress, addictions; the modern world is killing us. It's not appendicitis that finishes you, it's the addiction to your prescribed painkillers.

> 'I always take life with a pinch of salt. Plus a slice of lemon, and a shot of tequila.'
>
> *Unknown*

The game-changer is to grasp the slippery WWF wrestler that is 'happiness' and pin it down long enough to get a real good look into the whites of its eyes. If you're lucky, you'll see it. There's much more of this later in the book but for now you need to know that happiness is created from the inside. All the feelings you've ever experienced have been manufactured from within. That means everything is reversed. It gets a bit weird. The things that you thought made you happy – they actually don't.

Your pizza has lashings of mozzarella and pepperoni, but no actual happiness, not in the dough or the topping. Same with cake, your new car, phone upgrade, and number of social media followers.

happiness is made from... Thoughts!

oh!

Happiness is not some secret ingredient that exists in the outside world. You don't have to sit on a gluten-free cushion to feel good. Happiness is not an actual 'thing', you can't put it into a wheelbarrow, it's created entirely in your thoughts.

Then, just as you think you've grasped it, happiness has oiled itself up and wriggled away again. You feel as though you nearly got it but the slipperiest of concepts is gone, taunting you from somewhere over there. 'Come and get me baby.'

What's a happiness researcher to do other than roll up his sleeves and continue the stalking process?

Of course, most people aren't happiness researchers. They're normal people. The slippery customer that is an oiled-up WWF wrestler is but a figment of my imagination, dreamed into existence to make the point of elusiveness. The vast majority of people go about their day-to-day business without any of this crossing their minds. I think it's called ignorant bliss. Indeed, ignorance of ignorance must be the key to total bliss!

And that, right there, is pretty much the exact problem. It's not the slippery nature of what I'm trying to say, it's the fact that almost nobody ever tries to figure it out. Do you ever catch yourself thinking about thinking, reality, happiness, and the fact that we might actually be living in a *Matrix*-style self-generated parallel universe? That we're made up of molecules that are aware of molecules?

Of course you bloody well don't!

You've not got time for one thing, what with the modern hurly-burly of life. And when you do get a moment to think, it's thinking what you're going to do next. And then after that.

Hence the vast majority of people live their entire lives in the mistaken belief that the external world is making them feel the way they do.

Hedonism is the posh term for instant happiness, the quick fixes of chocolate, sex, alcohol, shopping, fast food, a line of coke, an armful of heroin, a lungful of crack – cram those into a night out and you'll be overflowing with joy. The problem with instant happiness is that you might be struggling for joy the next day. Over-consumption of things that bring instant joy will in fact bring long-term unhappiness. Ask someone sleeping in a shop doorway how their heroin happiness habit is going and you'll see the same pain in their eyes that is etched into their veins.

It's sometimes referred to as the hedonic treadmill – the relentless and never-ending pursuit of more. Just like a normal treadmill, it'll exhaust you. Indeed, too much instant happiness can kill you.

The Greeks came up with an alternative concept of happiness, 'eudaimonia', a complicated sounding word that more or less translates as 'the good life' in which we mix pleasure with purpose and meaning. Living the good life means knowing when to stop. It means saying no to some of the hedonistic urges, forgoing instant happiness in favour of long-term pleasure.

Hedonism versus eudaimonia has been a philosophical debate raging through the ages. Aristotle had a go, and Gandhi. I can't match their eloquence so here it is in Andy language:

Hedonism (instant happiness) is lashings of cake and sado-masochistic sex at the same time ('lashings', see what I did there?).

Eudaimonia (a good life) is S&M but with comfy handcuffs and a slice of cake *afterwards*.

Or, said in a slightly different way: in the long run, a deep and loving relationship will make you happier than a frenzied orgy.

There you go. That's pretty much what Gandhi meant to say. Maybe? Or when you stop chasing the wrong things you give the right things a chance to catch you.

Amen.

You Want Fries With That?

Ever fancied boiled frog? Kermit and fries? Me neither.

So here's an experiment NOT to try at home. Apparently, if you pop a frog into a pan of boiling water it will, not unsurprisingly, leap straight out. Hopping mad, I would imagine (sorry).

But if you place said frog in a pan of cold water and gradually heat it up, the frog will not jump out. Kermit will, in fact, boil to death.

Odd that.

I adore the modern world. We can send people into space. We can split atoms. We've created cat food that comes in individual gourmet sachets. We can cure diseases and replace worn out body parts. Messrs 'Wi' and 'Fi' have teamed up to invent invisible magical beams of stuff and Samuel Sung churns out handheld devices that tune into that invisible jiggery-pokery allowing you to access all the information in the world. And who knows, one day in the future, maybe it's not totally beyond the wit of someone to invent screens for those devices that don't actually smash.

My point? The modern world, generally speaking, is a wonderful place. If I had to pick any time or place to be born from the whole of history, it would be Derbyshire, today.

However …

The world has gradually been gathering pace. Not literally. If you observed our solar system from afar, our bluey-green rock is hurtling around the sun at a steady 67,000 mph, suspended in our galaxy which is, itself, moving at 1.3 million mph.

But that's nothing compared to the speed of human life. If you zoom in, society has speeded up. It's changed rapidly and seismically. Life, for the majority, is full on.

The norm is no longer the norm. There are lots of Kermits, boiling to death.

I don't feel old but I must be. I'm not *old* old. I'm old enough for nose and ear hairs to be a problem but not old enough to stop caring about them, but I am old enough to remember the 1970s and 80s, hence this book is peppered with references that millennials might not get.

Adults are very 'knowing'. All older generations, ever, have looked at the modern crop of youngsters and tutted. Let me give you an example. I deliver in schools and was recently working with some 14-year-olds in Warrington. Sixty in the group. Great kids. At breaktime every single one was on their phone. I'm talking EVERY SINGLE child. For EVERY SINGLE minute of breaktime. They were swapping clips, Instagramming, WhatsApping, texting, looking at videos of cats. It wasn't silent. They were chatting and giggling, whilst all the time looking at their screens. The lack of eye contact was a bit eerie. Because I'm 51. It's hard not to tut. I know better. I wouldn't do that.

But, of course, I absolutely would. If I was 14, I'd be doing exactly the same. What am I going to be, the one kid who sits there trying to make eye contact and chat about the social injustices implied in Orwell's *Animal Farm*? If so, I'm going to get bullied. To be fair, it'll probably be online and if

I'm the only kid not online then I'll never know. Because, in the modern world even bullying has moved to cyberspace. Kids don't stand toe to toe and punch seven bells out of each other anymore, while their peers gather and chant, baying for blood.

Nope. Blood-wise, it's a lot cleaner. They beat seven bells out of them on social media and while in the olden days your bloody nose and black eye

> 'Nostalgia isn't what it used to be.'
> *Ashleigh Brilliant (among others)*

would heal, the mental wounds of modern day bullying will stick around a lot longer. Whoever said 'sticks and stones will break my bones but words will never hurt me' clearly had no access to Facebook, Twitter, or Snapchat.

My teenage son actually watches YouTube videos of people playing computer games. It seems odd to me, although clearly not to him, that he'd prefer to watch others playing rather than play himself.

Hang in there while I make a terrifying leap to loving relationships and sex. There are an increasing number of men who have become immune to loving relationships. It's dysfunctional. Erectilely so. They've watched so many extreme acts that when they're actually centre stage with a real person it's lights, camera, but no action.

Are we consuming so much pornography that real flesh-on-flesh lovemaking is somehow less appealing? I don't know the answer, nobody does. Yet. I'm just daring to pose the question.

So as an 'old' person I can tut at the modern generation and their smartphone addiction all I like. It's what kids do. If I was them I would be doing it too. It's no good telling me to be different. You do what your peers do. End of!

Except it's not just kids, is it? Research out *this very day* suggests that adults check their phone every 18 minutes and within two minutes of waking up. And at night time when you're tucked up beside the love of your life, you're not sneaking your hand up their jimjams, you're stealing a sneaky peak at your emails and sending the world a goodnight tweet. #FFS

Three Horsemen and a Roadrunner

I used to love Looney Tunes' classic Roadrunner cartoons. Wile E. Coyote was so desperate to catch the fleet-footed bird that he'd do almost anything – magnets, bombs, nets, boulders rolled down hills – he was a very creative hound. In one episode he took delivery of an Acme robot roadrunner, a sexy female one with big eyelashes, in an attempt to lure his intended lunchtime snack into a trap. Epic failure.

But the all-time classic episode is where the desperate dog straps himself to a giant rocket, waits for the Roadrunner to *meep-meep* past, fixes his goggles into place, lights the fuse and whooooosh! He catches up until he's actually flying alongside the elusive bird. He can sniff his lunch … then as the bird follows a bend in the road the rocket goes straight ahead, over a cliff. The rocket splutters to a halt and Wile E. looks bloodshot-eyed to camera, suspended in thin air before animated gravity takes hold.

The classic cartoonery is aped in real life, except I doubt that very many people feel like the Roadrunner, speeding ahead, obliviously carefree and unaware of the traps along the way. Most of us can easily identify as the weary coyote, trying everything, even stupid tactics, that we hope will get us ahead. That momentary realization – the bloodshot eyes to camera look as another week slips by in near-exhaustion – we wear that look well.

But a lazy Wiki search throws up an interesting fact; coyotes are actually faster than roadrunners. So all those rockets, nets, bombs, and magnets weren't needed. All Wile E. Coyote needed to do was run. No need for bloodshot eyes, being impaled into the side of a mountain, or falling off a cliff. The solution was the most obvious thing in the world. That crazy coyote had gone and done what all of us do every single day – he'd overcomplicated things.

He'd accidentally become his own worst enemy.

As have we. In a brutal re-enactment of a Wild West scene, we're on the end of a rope being dragged through town by the three horsemen of the modern mental illness apocalypse: busyness, infomania, and musterbation. To clarify:

Busyness, aka 'blue-arsed fly syndrome', defined by Dictionary.com as 'lively but meaningless activity'.

Buzz

"Blue"

we've contracted 'blue - arsed fly Syndrome'

Infomaniac: a person who thrives and exists based on knowledge of facts (usually useless ones), much like a nymphomaniac relies on sex. Don't know the answer? Don't ponder, just Google it.

Musterbation: when you turn something you'd like to have into something you absolutely MUST have.

No wonder we're knackered! We're all stark raving infomaniacs, rushing around, musterbating like crazy. Overconsumption is killing us. It's like Suggs walking up your garden path; the first sign of madness.

Waiting for a train? Friend a bit late? Sitting on the toilet?[3] It's easy to spend this otherwise seemingly wasted time unlocking your smartphone screen and just triple-checking what's occurring. Oooh look! Three new emails, 14 people have liked this morning's Tweet, four Facebook messages, three new friend requests, someone's been at their job for 10 years on LinkedIn and I need to let the world know that my train's delayed by five minutes. Before

---

[3] One in five people have dropped their phone down the toilet. FACT!

you know it, those five minutes have been hoovered up and you're satisfied because you've not wasted them.

Get on your train, find your seat, and repeat.

All your nooks and crannies of time are filled.

> ## Modern definition
>
> 'Cellfish' (n): An individual who continues talking on their phone so as to be rude or inconsiderate of other people.

When I started my career emails hadn't been invented – 95% of our communication was done by talking. For the younger generation, our phones weren't mobile. At work you had one on your desk and at home, one in the hallway. One *between* us, along with a hefty phone book that listed everyone in your entire city. If you wanted a plumber, he'd be in the big yellow alternative.

The other 5% of communication was by memo – a workplace anachronism, in which you deposited a handwritten note into a tray and the magic admin fairy then delivered your handwritten note to whoever's name was on it. Then, 10 days later, you'd get a handwritten answer. You had a 'pigeonhole', a place that you had to physically go to, to collect your mail.

I know! Imagine? Ten days? The modern world can't wait 10 days! It can hardly wait 10 minutes! You sit there, emailing the person next to you, 'I'd like to talk to you but I haven't got time so I'm copying you into this email along with 67 other people, so I can't make them busy too …'

'I got a ransom note in the post. 'Pay us a million pounds or you'll never see your child again' and I couldn't believe it. Who still writes letters?'

Gary Delaney

I'm not saying the new world is better or worse, just faster and more immediate. If I want something new I can click and have it delivered the same day. My ready meal takes two minutes. I don't have to wait two weeks to get my photos developed, they're there, on screen, instantly. I don't have to wait until next week for the next episode of my fave TV series, I can binge on the entire series in a bulimic over-consumption of my favourite thing.

New relationship? Swipe, scroll, click. Sorted.

Modern media has always been based on the reselling of human attention to advertisers. The problem with human attention is that it invariably gravitates to the garish, titillating, outrageous, and negative.

'I started so many fights at my school – I had that attention-deficit disorder. So I didn't finish a lot of them.'

Simon Brodkin

Everything's been ramped up. 'Legend' has been devalued from 'slaying a dragon' to 'coming back from the bar with an unexpected bag of peanuts'. #WhatALedge

33

The UK tabloids have almost become a parody of themselves, falling over each other in the race to capture lurid celebrity headlines. Phone tapping, honey traps, and 'Elvis Alive and on the Moon'-style headlines lure us in. It's not just fake news, sometimes it's non-news that makes the best headline. ('Zip Me Up Before You Go Go' was the banner headline that ran after former pop star George Michael had been seen loitering around the gentlemen's toilets. Clever, but non-news.)

But hey, you're reading this, a proper book. You're clearly a reader of taste and sophistication. So no flimflam from me.

Okay, maybe a teeny bit. But not much though.

Those of us with problematic nose and ear hairs recall that we thought the technological revolution of the 1980s was information overload when, on reflection, it was a dripping tap. Nowadays we're being blown off balance by a fire-hose of information.

It's hard not to get suckered in. Yes, I've paid over the odds for some Nike trainers that have a secret ingredient, air. And yes, I've paid £40 for gold plated HDMI leads. And yes, I've paid a bit extra for a bottle of 'smart water'.

Our modern full-on existence means we're never really off. I have a nagging feeling that my smartphone is making me dumb. It's therefore worth pointing out something blindingly obvious: these online moments are your life. Clickbait is waiting, cheddar ready, to snare you. Tracking technology abounds. In a supreme internet irony *Slimming World*'s website has cookies. Free content is never really 'free'. It's costing us our sanity.

When you log on to social media and nibble the cheese you're snared for 90 minutes, clodhopping through clickbait to find out what your favourite soap star looks like now (clue, same but a bit older), it's not a time out from your actual life. The clock is not paused. Your 4000 weeks are not held in suspended animation while you absorb the trivia.

These minutes are your life!

You can't announce, 'Okay, I'm clicking pause while I crack on with my social media. I'm gonna check my usual webpages, then Tweets, then scroll on FB and 'like' a couple of Instagram stories. Then when I've done all that, I'll resume my life.'

Oh no no no. When you've done all the above, you'll resume your life alright, but it'll be 90 minutes shorter.

The realization is this: how you spend your minutes adds up to the sum total of how you spend your life.

> 'Tweeting on your day off is like beating a neighbour with a shovel. Not wrong, perhaps, but you should have better things to do.'
>
> *Philip Ardagh*

One of the British universities investigated compulsive gambling, internet addictions, and the excessive, perhaps even dangerous, use of social

35

networking sites. Technological compulsion like 'social media addiction' comes with all the behavioural signals that we might usually associate with chemical addictions, such as smoking or alcoholism. These include mood changes, social withdrawal, conflict, and relapse.

Is 'addiction' too strong a word? Am I over-egging it?

The problem with the world wide web is entanglement. An addiction is when you invest in an activity to the point of it becoming harmful. Drugs, alcohol, food, cigarettes – the harm is obvious and overt. Screen time is less obvious but I know people who are so engrossed in social media and/or video games that they neglect everything else in their lives.

Those teenagers from earlier? While my parents tutted about my long hair and denim jacket, they knew I'd grow out of it. My worry is born of the opposite; young people aren't going to grow out of smartphone addiction, they're getting more and more drawn into it. Look around and you'll see a host of anecdotal evidence; the rise of narcissism, an inability to make eye contact, a sense of having to compare with airbrushed perfection, a race to get more followers, the desire to be famous for the sake of being famous. Once these patterns are grooved into your mind, they're very difficult to shake off.

'People who use selfie sticks really need to have a good, long look at themselves.'

Abi Roberts

When you log on in a hotel or railway station you get a 'username'. You're therefore a 'user'. People who shoot up on heroin, they're 'users' too.

Look, I'm not ranting or stressing, merely pointing to something that we all know is coming. This is a bigger change than any of the 'next generation' huffing and puffing that has gone before.

Everything has what economists call an opportunity cost, the next best thing that you could have been doing. If, as surveys suggest, young people are spending nine hours a day on the internet (which incidentally is more time than they spend sleeping) then by age 80 they will have clocked up 30 solid years of wi-fi access.

Apart from being a sobering thought, that also carries a massive opportunity cost. It's 30 years that you could have spent making eye contact with real people, chatting to flesh and blood friends, eating ice creams, walking in the drizzle, watching sunsets, learning to play the piano, stroking a real cat, and making actual love (instead of watching others do it).

Social media is an echo chamber. Algorithms work out your preferences and give you news and products pertaining to what you already like. You never get to argue the opposite case. You never get to feel how other people feel, how people who aren't like you experience the world. The danger is that we become more polarized. We're like captive dolphins, deafened as our own sonar reverberates around us.

Remember Deresiewicz's 'most excellent sheep' from earlier? It's easy to be one of the flock. I think it's worth looking around at what everyone else is doing and NOT doing that.

My challenge to you is to be different, not a black sheep but a psychedelic one. A standout amazing sheep. The best in your field.

I don't want you to be so counter-intuitive that you stand out for the wrong reasons. There's a balance to be had and it's this; on balance, 30 years *not* spent online will likely yield more well-being and cultivate stronger relationships.

Bearded Wonder

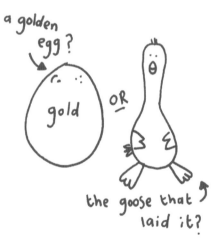

Several eons ago I started one of my books with a personal development question: what would you rather have, a golden egg, or the goose that laid it?

It was my pompous way of suggesting that *The Art of Being Brilliant* was somehow different to all the other books out there. Looking back, I was tuned into 'up my own arse FM'. Since then I've learned a whole load of stuff, and as a consequence, I'd like to disappear further into the dark crevasses of my nether regions.

This time there's no messing around. This book has a different starting point. It's not going to lay the occasional golden egg of personal development wisdom. I'm not even suggesting it's the goose that lays golden eggs of enlightenment.

I'm going much further by claiming that YOU ARE THE ACTUAL GOOSE!

#honk

That's quite a bizarre statement so I'll leave it hanging and return when the haze of understanding has been burned away by the sunshine of enlightenment.

Meantime, let's go dark. I'm a simple soul. Not simple as in 'village idiot' but as in 'uncomplicated'.

I've been off grid for a while. Deep cover. I've been inhabiting the murky world of the 'intellectual dark web' where academic skulduggery abounds. I've had to infiltrate the academic world, play their game, speak their lingo, wear elbow-patched jackets, learn their statistical techniques in order to become accepted as a boffin.

In the dark depths of academia there's something called the law of parsimony (otherwise known as 'Occam's Razor') which basically means the simplest theory is usually the best. That's why I love the paradox of Wiki's first line description: 'In science, Occam's razor is used as a heuristic guide in the development of theoretical models, rather than as a rigorous arbiter between candidate models.'

I've got no idea what 'heuristic' or 'rigorous arbiter' mean. In some lip-smackingly perverse twist of academic hokum, someone has managed to describe the science of simplicity in a way that is unfathomable to the masses.

Yet I am the masses. Infiltrating the academic world wasn't just deep cover, it was head-imploding Marianas Trench depths. For the record, it took me 12 years to get a PhD. I describe myself as a recovering academic. I've been coshed in dark doctoral alleyways, assaulted and battered by the big words police.

I've wandered down many academic cul-de-sacs that have been interesting dead ends. I've discovered stuff that's insanely attention-grabbing but that hasn't made the final cut for my Greatest Hits.

For example, statistically speaking, you are more likely to die on the way to buy a lottery ticket than you are to win the lottery itself. Or that it's physically impossible for a pig to look up at the sky. Did you know that a jiffy is an actual unit of time; 33.3564 picoseconds to be precise (the amount of time it takes light to travel a centimetre) or that all polar bears are left-handed? Every single one of them. I guess that explains why you never see them with scissors?

#Fact: It's scientifically proven that people who have more birthdays actually live longer. Cows can go upstairs but not downstairs, that's crazy right? The electric chair was invented by a dentist; no surprises there. Men with a bad sense of smell have small willies. Really? Yep. But that nugget doesn't make it into this book. Neither does the fact that the happiest temperature is 20°C [68°F], so you're more likely to find happiness in Manchester than Miami.

Here's another belter; according to the *Journal of the American Medical Association*, medical treatment is the third-leading cause of death after heart disease and cancer in the United States. Let that last one settle for a few seconds. Vast numbers of people are dying from medical treatment.

And then there are facts that aren't facts. *Unfacts!* The sun rises in the east and sets in the west … not true. The sun isn't rising and setting, it's us, the earth, that's rotating to give the illusion of a rising and setting sun.

I'm giving you these gems as castaways – freebies – things I've found along the way but that haven't made it into this book! I'm tossing them aside to make room for life-enhancing content, academic elixir that's been filtered through the finest of meshes that extracts the bullshit and psychobabble. I've left that sediment for other authors. You've spent a tenner on my book. You deserve the purified best.

Here's one I know you're going to love: the Dunning–Kruger effect – the phenomenon of less-intelligent people being more confident. Dunning and Kruger were inspired by reports of a criminal who held up banks after covering his face with lemon juice. Why would you do that? Because lemon juice can be used as invisible ink, so he thought his face wouldn't show up on camera, that's why.

Once again, you might have to let that one sink in for a few seconds.

He actually really thought that.

Dunning–Kruger[4] is a re-working of ignorance being bliss. If you don't know very much, there's not much to be afraid of.

Sure, I've managed to bag myself a PhD but that doesn't make me a boffin, unless you judge me via Einstein's definition that genius is 1% inspiration and 99% perspiration. If locking yourself away in a library for 12 years and working yourself beyond the level you were originally designed for is genius, then I will take a bow.

I've slogged so you don't have to. I'm deadly serious about happiness. Yes, ladies and gentlemen, I am indeed a Doctor of

[4] J. Kruger and D. Dunning (1999) Unskilled and unaware of it: How difficulties in recognizing one's own incompetence lead to inflated self-assessments. Journal of Personality and Social Psychology, 77(6), 1121–34.

Happiness. I wear the Doctor of Happiness masquerade ball costume, but behind the mask it's just me, a bloke from Derby. Ordinary in every way, and proudly so.

So I'll end Part 1 with another academic gem. Silvia Bellezza surveyed students to see which university professors they perceived as most intelligent. Her findings? Students rated the bearded and tee-shirted ones as having 14% more brainpower than the clean-shaven shirt and tie ones.[5]

First up, the bearded thing, I'm assuming it was a study of male professors?

Second, the reason the bearded tee-shirted ones were bestowed with boffin status was because the standard dress code was 'business', so smart was the norm. Those who dared to buck the trend gained what are called 'idiosyncrasy credits' – a subconscious points allocation from those around you.

This book has been six months in the making. It only took two days to write but the other five months and 29 days were spent waiting for my beard to grow to 'academic proportions'. I didn't have time to wait for the Dumbledore look, but I promise you, it's a decent bird's nest and is worn with a faded AC/DC tee-shirt.

By Bellezza's standards, I look proper clever.

Part 1 has been scene setting. Monocle fixed in place, off we trot to Part 2, some science …

----

[5] S. Bellezza, G. Francesca, and K. Anat (2014) The surprising benefits of nonconformity. MIT Sloan Management Review, 55(3), 10–11.

Part 2

THE HUMAN OPERATING SYSTEM

emotional
creature

Welcome to the second instalment, in which we up the academic ante by introducing the science of happiness and revelry. But we have to take the long route, via some prior knowledge, otherwise when we arrive, the science means nowt.

So brace yourself for some emotional spillage and a trip down memory lane to when Raquel Welch gave birth to the human race. These were ancient times when the dogs bow-wow-wowed, we went wild in the country, and the snakes in the grass were absolutely free.

Then we get you in a vice-like grip and pop your bonnet to reveal a whole tangled mess of spam and Nigerian princes. I explain why dogs don't take themselves for walkies and why zebras don't get ulcers.

Then it's all flashbacks, phobias, and the unearthing of a gorgeous 1970 lost gem of a cartoon called *Captain Caveman and His Enormous Chopper*.

Part 2 opens a can of worms that will be fully cranked in Part 4. The early wrigglers are the introduction to your 'happy place' as well as dumbfounding you with the age-old chicken and egg conundrum (plot spoiler, 100% definitely the egg).

There's an entertaining aside about what I'm calling the 'Normal Olympics' (not the 'paranormal') but the best bit is the end. I do solemnly swear that it's worth hanging in there, through the lumpy custard of science, to the folklore that follows. If authors are allowed favourite bits, the castle full of bearded psychological munchkins has to be it.

Thank you for getting this far. May the force stay with you.

Part 2 is brought to you by the word **Tsavd danem**. Armenian /
int. / tsæv danem / tsav dah-nem. Lit. 'let me take away your
pain'; used in various ways to position the speaker as interested
in/caring about the other.

Emotion Creates Motion

Basics first. Humans are emotional creatures. Everything you do
you do for a feeling and, at the most basic level, we're driven
towards good feelings and away from bad ones.

The thing about emotions is that they're hugely important, but
not actually real. By that, I mean emotions aren't a 'thing' at all,
they don't have a form or a shape. You can't put your feelings
in a wheelbarrow and cart them around. They're triggered by
events 'out there' but exist as mental construct, in your head.

You created them.

That's first base. Next up, our superior brains give us massive
processing power but they are also constructed to facilitate the
transfer of emotions. This puts us in line with just about every
species on the planet. If I'm walking my mutt and she sniffs a
rabbit, the bunny's off like a rocket, white tail bobbing, alerting
all the other rabbits to scamper too.

We are biologically driven to mimic others outwardly and, in
mimicking their outward displays, we also end up adopting

their inner states. At its simplest level, someone smiles because they feel happy – you mimic the smile and also feel happy.

The contagious nature of emotion plays a big part in our survival – one hunter feels fear and the others tread more carefully as a result – it all makes perfect evolutionary sense. Emotional contagion also helps us build communities and relationships; love, empathy, happiness; these bind us together.

This 'emotional spillage' creates a ripple effect that reaches three degrees of people removed from you. On a good day your positivity bubbles over, creating an uplift in those around you. And on a *reaaaaally* good day you are a mini emotional Vesuvius, sending an ash of joy that settles on people far and wide.

Bottom line? You, in TGI Friday mode, are positively impacting on your friends, your friends' friends, and your friends' friends' friends.

If we apply the ripple effect to a simple situation – say, the workplace – you coming in full of genuine enthusiasm and positivity will resonate with your work colleagues. They will experience an upward spiral of emotions simply because you're in their life.

49

But it doesn't stop there. Your work colleagues then go home to their families and because they're feeling great, their family is now benefiting from your positivity.

But it doesn't stop there either! One of those family members pops out to the supermarket and has some banter with the lady on the checkout and she's now feeling more positive.

Just to be clear, you haven't met your work colleagues' family or the lady on the checkout, but all of those people are feeling great because of you. Your joie de vivre has leaked! It's your gift to the world and oh so simple.

So why the heck do we reserve our happiness for Fridays? Why not TGI Mondays? It's a seventh of our lives we've learned to loathe. Why is our species so negative? Why are there so many human Vesuvius's belching out black clouds and poisonous gas instead?

The Evolution of Negative

When we look around at our abundant lives, it's easy to forget that our ancestors eked out a meagre living. We're only the second or third generation who have access to unlimited food, central heating, sit-down jobs, and modern healthcare. Even now, that's not a global proposition. It's a shattering fact that if you're a nurse in the UK, that puts you in the top 1% of earners globally.

Go back a few hundred years and you'll find that people lived in small groups. It was very uncommon to meet someone you didn't know and often dangerous when you did. Couple that with parasites, injury, no prescription drugs, no police – the world really was a dangerous place.

So many current issues are a throwback. Ever wondered why you love fatty and sugary foods? Because, not that long ago, your family's food supply was unreliable. Fat helped us bulk up, in preparation for months of scarcity. A sugary taste was the sign that the berries were not going to kill us.

Fast forward to today and fatty and sugary foods still trigger the reward and pleasure circuits in our brains. We crave more of what we know is bad for us. Everyone knows the truth about food and exercise. The logic is easy but remember, we're *emotional* creatures. After I've had a heavy night out my wife doesn't blink her way downstairs to find out what the noise is all about, only to find me crashing around in mid preparation of a 'comfort salad'.

Our brains are a paradox of refined sophistication built upon an original Neanderthal processor. The contents of your skull were moulded by the need to survive and reproduce. Your grey matter evolved with a hair-trigger readiness to react to danger. In fact, from a survival standpoint, if you failed to heed danger there would be no tomorrow.

Let me bring some colour to this very grey matter via a trip back down memory lane. This is an important bit so put your best furrowed brow on, and focus.

Humans are a weird set of contradictions. First up, almost everyone has the belief that the future will be much better than the past and present. We keep peering into the distance through our 'finer future goggles' because there's a rosy glow on the horizon. Like moths to a light, we flutter that-a-way, towards a pot of emotional gold, a big helping of happiness, at the far end of the rainbow.

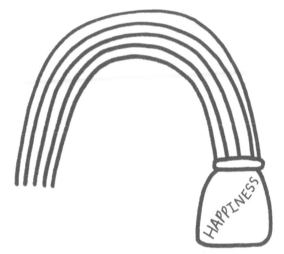

You'd perhaps expect folk who are glum right now to imagine that things might pick up, but even people who are stupendously happy right now still expect their happiness to be even greater five years hence. This pattern of expecting the future to be brighter than today affects almost everyone so it's not a quirk, it's very much part of the human way and, of course, academics have a name for it, 'positive illusions'.

Although these mental biases are incorrect (sadly, your happy tomorrow is like the real tomorrow – it never actually arrives), they serve an important evolutionary purpose.

To understand why we're constructed with such an optimistic future satnav, it's worth considering the repercussions for our species if our brains had the opposite software. Imagine, just for a second, that human minds were constructed to be 'very happy now' and 'much less happy in the future'. We'd be scared stiff of moving forward. Humans would stop striving and civilization would grind to a halt. We would literally cease to evolve. If the future is predicted to be worse than the present, our ancestors would never have ventured far from their tribes and we might all be cave dwellers, still huddled together in the cold, thinking this was as good as it gets.

So, I get it. Our species is driven forwards by 'positive illusions', which are essentially a collection of happiness mirages that stop us throwing the towel in.

The brow-furrowing bit is therefore this: if optimism is built into our system, how is it that the voice in your head is so negative?

It's rather a technical point that might only be of interest to the purist but I'll explain it anyway. It seems that optimism is reserved for your 'future goggles' so you're scanning the horizon through a rose-tinted glow.

Sadly, your 'now goggles' don't have the same pink hue. The horizon might be glowing with brilliance but the present moment, Fatboy Slim's 'right here, right now', is often tinged with disappointment, unrest, regret, and minor irritation.

Your future-focused 'positive illusions' are counterbalanced by the gravitational pull of so-called 'negativity bias'. It might be bright on the horizon but we're driving around like the Gruesome Twosome in *Wacky Races*. If you recall, their 'creepy coupe' had a full-time black cloud swirling around.

So why has evolution equipped us to see happiness on the horizon but negativity in the moment? More about 'now' later (I've been waiting a lifetime to write those four words) but meantime, it's worth examining why 'now' is so shit (those words are pretty cool too).

The reason we're tuned into negatives is that positives are less pressing. As Jon Haidt reminds us, we have been sharing this planet with all sorts of creatures that can eat, sting, bite, and even electrocute us for the best part of 200,000 years. The only thing that has changed in the last few hundred years is us: large-scale deforestation and expanding urbanization have wiped out or marginalized entire species that previously posed a danger to our existence. The wolves and bears that once roamed Stevenage, they're more or less gone.

To make the point, let's play a simple game that's fun for everyone except me. Let's take two versions of me and send them back several millennia to when the world really was full of bitey, stingy, eaty predators. The only upside is that Raquel Welch is marauding around in her mammoth skin bikini.[1]

---

[1] Political correctness hadn't been invented 1 million years BC, which was the title of the film. Hence my referring to Raquel's bikini is perfectly fine.

First, let's live a day as the cautious me, a nailed-on pessimist. My morning is spent on the arduous chores of de-lousing and trying to invent the wheel. Then I'm allocated foraging duties. My elders want nuts and berries as a bare minimum. If I can spear a piglet, we'll be dancing around the campfire that evening. I don my sabretooth thong and off I go, spear raised, wandering in the long grass. This hyper-vigilant version of me hears some rustling in the undergrowth and takes evasive action. Steering well clear of the bush, the venomous snake goes back to sleep and I return home with berries and a suckling pig.

Raquel thinks I'm a hero. There's the tiniest glimmer that one day she'll want to share a cave with me and my genes will be fortunate enough to pass on.

Let's live the same day as the happy-go-lucky ultra-optimistic me. Instead of de-lousing I sit and watch some cloud formations floating by. I've invented mindfulness but little do I know that the lice have laid eggs and are burrowing into my skin, ready to hatch next week. That actually doesn't matter because I'm not going to live that long anyway.

The carefree me is assigned the same foraging duty so I skip off into the wilderness, scratching, whistling, and perhaps singing. Zip-a-dee-doo-dah hasn't been invented so I'm yabba dabba doo-ing and heading out for a gay old time.

The viper rustles in the bush, warning me off. The happy, optimistic me thinks it might be a fluffy bunny rabbit so I part the leaves, peer in, and that's the end. Instead of bringing home the bacon, I am the bacon.

Raquel makes eyes at someone else and it's his genes that pass on, not mine.

This 'silly' example is far from silly. This kind of thing has happened millions of times over thousands of generations. Pessimism, alertness, scanning for danger, planning for the worst – these are the neural pathways etched into the human brain.

The fact that happiness enhances your life but doesn't save it is a crucial evolutionary adaptation. It means we are ninjas of negativity. Cut to today and the dangers have receded but the same brain circuitry is continually scanning for danger. Indeed, Evan Gordon suggests the brain scans the environment five times a second, looking for danger. This is just the way it is.

It's not just you, it's the human race. But just because that's the way it is, doesn't mean that's the way it *has* to be. It's like having an iPhone and just sending texts. Your brain is capable of so much more, once you learn how.

Under the Hood

If we strapped you into a Black & Decker Workmate and took a circular saw to your skull, we'd tease you open and beneath the bonnet you'd be running millions of mental algorithms, weighing up information, sifting data, comparing situations with what's gone before, calculating possibilities, and coming to solutions in the blink of an eye.

Flipping the bonnet, we'd see a tangled mess of habits, traits, outdated connections, and inefficient systems. Your brain didn't happen overnight, it gradually evolved over millions of years to reach this current level of complexity, but as a result it has accrued a great deal of add-ons. No matter how much you try and reboot, some of the old pop-ups continue to pop up, spoiling your experience as they do.

Our brains are organized in exactly the *opposite* way to your computer's spam filter. You pay an annual subscription for some clever software to stop all the crappy emails coming at you. Sure, some Nigerian millionaires slip through with their generous requests for you to swap your bank details for a percentage of the fortune their mum left them, but by and large, 90% of the spammy stuff is sent to an email holding pen. It's blocked. Your inbox is busy, but with good stuff.

Your brain isn't a spam filter, it's a spam *filler*. All the metaphorical Nigerian princes are calling at your door. Your brain is alert to every threat, crisis, and potential embarrassment. In fact, it's so finely tuned towards negativity that if there isn't a crisis it's very good at imagining one.

This bias towards negativity is your default operating system. Although sabretooths and packs of hungry dogs are pretty much eradicated from modern life (except in parts of Lincolnshire) your brain is still on alert. That's why one bad driver ruins your entire commute, one angry customer spoils your day, and you remember the one bad episode (the one with the fly) from the five series (62 episodes, thank you Wiki) of *Breaking Bad*.

There's something amazing about the human capacity to think. If we have more or less the same DNA as a mouse, why can't a mouse, say, invent a new type of cheese? Or why can't sheep shear themselves? Instead of waiting (and waiting and waiting) for their long necks to evolve, why didn't giraffes invent step ladders? Monkeys, our closest cousins – why haven't they learned to write music and choreograph shows? Why haven't squirrels invented apps that help them remember where they stored their nuts? Why don't dogs take themselves for a walk? Why don't palomino horses run for parliament?

They're missing the missing link, an evolutionary brain adaptation that's allowed humans to rule the world.

Did you know that zebras don't get ulcers? Not only did you not know it, but truth be told you didn't want to know it. But hey-ho, now you do. I may as well explain.

Humans have experienced a relatively recent mental upgrade. The bit above your eyebrows. In fact, if you put both hands to your head as you would if your team concedes a last-minute goal (please do this, even if you're reading on a train. To add some spice, you can also adopt the face, à la Edvard Munch's The Scream.)

Thank you.

Your prefrontal cortex is exactly that bit.

This bit of the brain differentiates us from, say, lizards. That and their scaly skin and ability to lay eggs. Oh, and the flicky-out tongue thing. Our neurological upgrade allows us to reflect on the past, to dream about the future, to make plans, and, best of all, to imagine things that aren't there.

That's amazing, but also a curse. Our brains are large enough to torment us. Let me explain via the medium of zebras. These stripy horses don't have a prefrontal cortex. I'm assuming that's why they never go to football matches. That last-minute goal thing, the zebra would literally not know that it had to put its hooves to its head and adopt 'that' face.

Imagine a zebra, tail swishing, head down, munching on the grasslands of the African savannah. Always alert, the zebra spies a lion springing from the long grass. Adrenaline kicks in, the zebra legs it, running faster than it knew it could, until it manages to outrun the lion. The big cat slinks back to the long grass, mane ruffled and tummy a-rumbling, a sure sign that the lion won't sleep tonight. Its pride has been hurt in all senses of the phrase.

Within 60 seconds of feeling safe, our chubby black and white equine will resume its tail swishing, head down, chomping away at the grass. The lion's gone. Panic over. Move on.

Now, just for a moment, imagine that you're on holiday somewhere in the African savannah and you catch sight of a lion emerging from the long grass. It's prowling. The zebra has escaped its jaws so it's doubly determined to get a tasty steak – a human rump. You drop your camera and run, zebra-like, faster and further than you thought possible. Eventually, lungs

59

busting and sweat patches merging into each other, you lean against a tree, remove your pith helmet and mop your brow. It's been a skin-of-your-teeth experience but you've escaped.

You'd return home, traumatized. You'd visit your GP and be prescribed something for your anxiety and panic attacks. Your brain would replay the 'lion incident' over and over again, waking you up with 3am cold sweats. You'd become wary of your own domesticated mog, you'd have time off work with a diagnosed 'big cat phobia' and although you love Disney's Timon and Pumbaa you know you'll never be able to watch them again. Likewise BBC wildlife documentaries. Just in case.

So the human brain is a magnificent piece of kit that's allowed us to take over the world. We are masters of the universe, but it's come at a price. Our ability to think is killing us. More specifically, our *over*thinking, and in some cases, it's literally killing us. My lion example is but a childlike way of alluding to a deep-seated human problem. Our thoughts are causing us to jump off tall buildings or in front of trains.

The mix of sociology and chemistry is insanely interesting. Criticisms, insults, rejections, mockery – these external events create a rush of the stress hormone, cortisol, which assaults our sense of self-worth, especially if done publicly. This interferes with our goal of being liked and accepted.

Nice things, such as receiving praise, also produce a neurological reaction, the warm glow of oxytocin which conjures pleasure and pride.

But chemically, these hormones aren't equal. Oxytocin (the nice warm glowing stuff) is removed from your bloodstream in about five minutes whereas cortisol (the jagged, edgy chemical) can linger for a couple of hours.

It means the good feelings get washed away while painful ones linger.

How unfair is that?

Hippopotomonstrosesquipedaliophobia

We've all got baggage. Anyone who reaches the ripe old age of 30 has endured enough personal disasters, relationship faux pas, and embarrassing moments to ruin the rest of your life.

If you let them.

My childhood was generally pretty good but I'm getting flashbacks to the child abuse I suffered when I was a choir boy in the Catholic Church.

And that's odd because I wasn't a choir boy, I never actually went to church, and I certainly wasn't touched.

My naughty little gibe is designed to make a wider point about being saturated in societal suffering. Eckhart Tolle[2] calls it the 'pain-body', your resident well of sorrow that can be triggered at any time. Tolle's point is that the pain-body is not

----

[2] E. Tolle (2009) A New Earth. London: Penguin.

just individual in nature. It runs through societies and through history, passed down via tribal stories. Human history is a big book of tribal warfare, enslavement, pillage, rape, torture, suppression, violence, famine, and injustice. This pain still lives in the collective psyche of humanity and is being added to on a daily basis, as you can verify when you watch the news tonight or look at the drama in people's relationships.

We're at a point in history where governments are paying compensation for historical wrongdoing, where the descendants of the done-tos are suffering even though they weren't the ones wrongly done to. History has hitch-hiked into the present via stories, rituals, and culture.

As a Brit, I'm thinking of sticking in a claim against those bastard Vikings.

Emotions exist for a reason. All of them have positive intent. Fear, for example, is there to protect you. Anger is also a perfectly valid emotion. It primes your nervous system so you're ready to attack or defend yourself.

> 'Fear is useful. It stops us doing stupid things. Without fear we would have tigers as pets and we would juggle chainsaws for giggles. That might not work out well for some.'
>
> Chris Baréz-Brown

So is there such a thing as a 'negative emotion'?

Yes, there most certainly is. A negative emotion is one that is toxic to the body and interferes with its balance and harmonious functioning. Fear, anxiety, anger, bearing a grudge, sadness, hatred, intense dislike, jealousy, envy – they all serve you well in short bursts but if they're your normal way of getting through the day, you'll be experiencing disrupted energy flows, heart murmurs, an exhausted immune system, digestive problems, and a whole range of internal machinations that can be unspeakably bad.

Modern society has become expert at putting us on the edge of mental illness. There are 7.5 billion of us, teetering. We're all on the social anxiety spectrum, but if you get to the point where your foibles are actually disruptive, that's when they become diagnosable disorders. Some of these are common and totally understandable, such as arachnophobia (fear of spiders), acrophobia (heights), trypanophobia (needles), glossophobia (public speaking), and bullshitophobia (politicians).

If you scratch around there are plenty of obscure ones that sound good fun but probably aren't. Note, these are all true: pogonophobia (fear of beards), omphalophobia (belly buttons), alektorophobia (chickens), Paraskevidekatriaphobia (fear of Friday the 13th – about 8% of Americans have this apparently), turophobias (cheese) and what must be the worst of the worst, panophobia, the fear of everything.

To prove that psychologists are evil bastards the fear of long words is called hippopotomonstrosesquipedaliophobia. It really is. Plus they've invented phobophobia, the fear of having a phobia.

Bunkum and nonsense perhaps? Unless you've got some of them, in which case an invite to cheese and wine in Bearded Pete's 64th floor apartment on Friday 13th where you're going to have to say a few words – that's a full house and BINGO, you've got full-blown 'pano'.

Phobias are your brain going haywire, working yourself up into a frenzy. Often phobics know the illogical nature of their fear. For instance, coulrophobics understand that clowns are just normal people with face paint, but they ain't ever going to a circus.

If you bought them a ticket their brain would activate all the 'likely' scenarios, and their fight-or-flight response would be activated. The brain's emotions centre, the amygdala, codes 'clowns' alongside 'terror' and that's good enough to trigger panic.

Yes, it's perfectly possible to get to the point where just *thinking* about clowns can bring on an attack.

Top tip:

What should you do if you're attacked by a gang of clowns?

Go for the juggler.

There's one aspect of the modern world that is having a particularly pernicious effect on happiness – social learning means we're wired to compare and contrast. You can't help it. The social self-preservation theory states that humans have a deep-rooted motivation to preserve their social standing and to continue being liked by the people whose approval they value.

It's our biggest hangover from way back. I read about an excavation in which 150 ancient bodies were dug up, along with 450 axes. The archaeologists noticed that nearly all were sharp-bladed with intricate handles.

It was puzzling. A hoard of unused but beautifully crafted axes had the archaeologists scratching their dusty craniums. Their conclusion was that the axes weren't for chopping or doing traditional axe-related stuff, they were crafted by the men as a means of attracting a female. Captain Caveman would spend hours making an axe that he would then hang above their fireplace, like an olden day 'do you want to pop in to see my etchings?'

Palaeolithic Pauleen would drop by for a bowl of gruel and swoon at the intricately carved handle. 'Ooo err Cavey, that's a mighty fine chopper. Much bigger than Igor's. Let's get married my love.' (I'm guessing. I wasn't there.)

Cut to modern times and we're still in the moreish race, pursuing faster, glitzier, better. The comparison ante has been well and truly upped, from 150 village idiots to 7.5 billion. Cavey v Igor has morphed into a global axe-fest. We trawl social media measuring up. Possessions, holidays, cars, family,

THE LITTLE BOOK OF BEING BRILLIANT

partner … choppers. In the global game of go-compare, keeping up with the other runners and riders, the Joneses, is a lung-busting impossibility.

How many miles has your thumb scrolled as you read post after post of other people's blue sky holidays, first-class-graduating offspring, perfect family gatherings, white wedding of the year, running a sub-three-hour marathon (and smiling to camera at the end) – and you think *what utter bastards!*

I promise you, that post-marathon smile was the only good bit of the entire 2 hours and 59 minutes. They haven't posted the grimacing, the cramp, or the bit where they shat their pants at mile 23. As Paul McGee so eloquently says, other people's grass might appear greener but quite often it's been fertilized with bullshit.

I'd add, as is your own.

We're all lured into the game. How many times have you been guilty of doing exactly the same thing, posting the best of the best of your iPhone pics, creating a social media world that's not quite as pristine from the inside as it seems on the outside?

Here's a thought to take us into the study of wellness and the science of human flourishing;

Psychosomatic disorders are ailments that have a mind-body connection. So if you can worry yourself ill, it must also be possible to un-worry yourself well. If we flip the emotional coin we find that there are such things as positive emotions which are good for you. They strengthen the immune system, invigorate, and repair the body.

So let's move on to these positive emotions, where do they come from and how can you feel them more often?

Your Happy Place

I was chatting to a head teacher who admitted she was really stressed but would be okay in three weeks because she'd be on holiday in her apartment in Spain. There was a particular beachside restaurant that she was looking forward to visiting. 'That's my happy place. I'll chill, destress and relax.'

She's got an actual place that she goes to to be happy.

I can't help thinking it's bordering on the lemon juice example. While I totally understand what she means, it's also totally ridiculous.

I'm going to grapple with this in Part 4, but it's worth opening the worm can and letting a few wriggle out. What she doesn't realize is that when she's in Spain she's giving herself a mental holiday, letting the feelings of busyness fall away, dropping her stress. Because she's not thinking work thoughts, they don't feature in her feelings.

It's less about the place where your feet are and more about the place your head is. Her 14 days in Spain is respite from her usual thinking but she's not 'cured'. As soon as she arrives home she's plunged straight back into busyness thinking.

67

just a few

Dr Sonia Lyubomirsky[3] (and others) maintain that only a thin sliver of your happiness is determined by what's going on around you. Hence your circumstances matter, but not nearly as much as you think they do. The totality of your circumstances (e.g. gender, ethnicity, traumas, triumphs, marital status, education level, health, income, physical appearance, and your lifestyle) accounts for only 10% of your happiness. This counter-intuitively is hard to believe to the point that Lyubomirsky herself has to go to pains to hammer it home: 'The general conclusion from almost a century of research on the determinants of wellbeing is that objective circumstances, demographic variables and life events are correlated with happiness less strongly than intuition and every day experience tell us they ought to be.'

The point is that by changing your outside circumstances you can influence 10% of your happiness. Yet that's the sliver that we focus most of our efforts on. We go to extraordinary

[3] S. Lyubomirsky (2001) Why are some people happier than others? The role of cognitive and motivational processes in wellbeing. American Psychologist, 56, 239–49.

lengths to create an external lifestyle that makes us happy. In the case of that head teacher she was working incredibly long hours to create enough money to buy things that will make her happy. She'd achieved her nirvana, an apartment in Spain. Her happy place.

A much bigger chunk of your happiness can be influenced by changing what's going on *inside* your head. Back to that head teacher again, she had bought peace and tranquillity for two weeks every year. In Spain. Without realizing that she could have Spain every day. In her head.

Unless you change your thinking, all you end up doing is bringing your internal world to the external environment. Guess what? You achieve brief respite but nothing changes!

Create the life that you want from the inside out. Do that first and you're more likely to create an external world that works for you.

Hang on. We need to ponder those sentences. They're so much bigger than they sound.

Here they are again: *Create the life that you want from the inside out. Do that first and you're more likely to create an external world that works for you.*

> 'You were only supposed to blow the bloody doors off.'
> Michael Caine. The Italian Job

The blowing the bloody doors off bit is that if you can find a way of creating inner happiness, the external world that you create might not be quite the luxury that you previously thought you needed.

Gosh, this is hard to keep simple! Maybe it's not the big house? Maybe it's not Spain? If the inside bit (your thinking) is right the external requirement is different from the one you originally imagined you would need.

One more go. I can't nail it any more simply than this: the moment you're content, you have enough.

Any clearer?

If I made you an offer – you can have £1m or not be dead – you'd be perplexed at the randomness of it but the silliness would be shrugged off with the obvious choice of 'not be dead', thank you very much.

I can upgrade you to £10m or £50m and you'd still go for the 'not be dead' option.

Yet we rarely wake up with that at the forefront of our minds. Here's some BREAKING NEWS: skipping out of bed, opening the curtains, looking at the drizzle and shouting 'Yippee, I'm alive' – that's not normal.

Forget the usual suspects; the Gandhis, Luther Kings, Kung Fu Pandas, and Mandelas. Michael Jackson, the prince of pop, was also a bit of a personal development guru. Our single-gloved, crotch-tweaking, no-nosed megastar believed that if you wanted to make the world a better place, you needed to take a look in the mirror and make that change. *Hoo!*

Hence, I want to introduce you to your very own happy place: your mind.

Chickens and Eggs

If you could be a superhero, but only on the condition that you have to be a new one, so no super strength, bionics, mind reading, speed, or invisibility, who would you be?

If the ensemble got a new cast member, I'd be Analogy Man: boldly spotting equivalences wherever he goes. Agreed, not the greatest movie, but if you listen carefully you might be able to hear him bashing around in his phone box, stepping into his Y fronts. Analogy Man's a real bastard because he sometimes makes you work things out for yourself.

Onwards … to 'get' positive psychology you have to be dumbfounded, my definition of which is to be founded by your dumbness. In other words, to be enlightened you need to admit you've been en-darkened for a very long time.

In the same way that 'realization' means that, up until now, you hadn't realized and 'awakening' means you've been in deep slumber.

To wake up, you need to realize there's more than a semantic difference between 'change' and 'transformation'.

Hark, is it a bird? Or a plane? No it's a bloke in underpants emerging from a phone box. Analogy Man would best describe it thus. Imagine you lived in an egg. Like Mork – I think he did. Anyway, it's a nice cosy, comfortable egg. 'Change' is about staying in your egg. Maybe you can paint your egg so it looks funky and decorate the inside so it's extra comfy and cosy. Change is tinkering with what already is. Note, being busy and being productive are two different things.

There are a lot of people, the tinkers, busy folk, in a perpetual state of change.

Transformation is different. It's about hatching.

In terms of psychology, we've been decorating our eggs for a long time. Academics build a body of knowledge that pushes the boundaries of what we already know. They publish their work and the academic who published a particular piece of work gets a month to swoon knowing full well that the other academics are in a jealous unpublished rage. So they do what's called 'peer review' which is shorthand for ripping your research to bits, picking holes in the methodology, sneering at your conclusions until your research is Swiss cheese.

And this goes on and on in an endless cycle of one-upmanship. As a result, the subject inches forward.

Then, at the back end of the 1990s, psychology transformed. It was a hatching of epic proportions and the guy who emerged from the egg, flapping his wings into the brave new world, was Professor Marty Seligman. I guess he's positive psychology's mother hen?

Instead of looking at existing psychological research and poo-pooing it, why not rethink the subject entirely and, instead of studying what's wrong with people, why not study what's right with them?

This isn't to say that all the research which has gone before is wrong – the scientific study of phobias, disorders, depression, anxiety, and the other 600 mental maladies is all aimed at easing the suffering. But what about those who aren't suffering? That handful of people you can think of, right now, who are flourishing. The happy ones. The smilers. With energy, optimism, enthusiasm, and vivacity.

Yes, the exact ones that psychology has never studied. What about doing some research on them?

This transformation of the subject sends you down the Alice in Wonderland rabbit hole into the warreny nether regions of consciousness, strengths, happiness, entropy, resilience, empathy, relationships, community,

'I was watching the London Marathon and saw one runner dressed as a chicken and another runner dressed as an egg. And I thought: 'This could be interesting.''

Paddy Lennox

and positive deviance. There was a bit of thrashing around in the psychological darkness for a while but, for a lot of us, the realization dawned that we'd stop rearranging our egg and had broken free into something vast. The science of glee. A world that was always there, but we were so fucking busy painting our eggs that the brave new world was hidden from sight.

Indeed the subject area of 'positive psychology' struggled and, in some quarters, is still flapping its fledgling wings. The ones painting their eggs have a lot of vested interest in inching the science of mental ill-health forward. The stark fact is that there are a lot of people employed in careers that are dependent on human misery. All mean well and most are gorgeously warm-hearted people.

However, in those circles there are a few hardcore die-hards who deride positive psychology as some sort of wishy-washy new age positive thinking fly-by-night that doesn't bear academic scrutiny. It's almost as though happiness, well-being, and positive emotions are less worthy of study than the heavyweights of depression and melancholia.

My first degree included a shedload of psychology. There was a lot of egg painting. Every lecture was named after a disorder. There was a whole term devoted to 'personality disorders' and over the three years we trawled all the genres of psychology: child, cognitive, addiction, clinical, educational, occupational, neuro, and social.

And, boy, have we become good at it! Since I left uni the boffins have invented a few new ways to paint the egg.

Forensic psychology, which includes criminal profiling as well as neglect and abuse cases. Cyberpsychology, the study of all the shit that can go wrong when you become addicted to wifi. Consumer psychology, used by marketing firms to tempt us into buying things we don't want, and geropsychology, associated with depression and disorders in old people.

Literally, from cradle to grave, we have a branch of psychology that will examine maladies, mental illnesses, and reasons to be cheerful. *Not.*

Pretty much forever psychology has been predicated on the question, how can we alleviate suffering? To alleviate suffering, you have to identify people who are struggling, find out why, and fix them.

So I became the UK's first psychological devil's advocate. I turned psychology on its head. What would happen if, for a change, we came at suffering from the other end of the spectrum? Starting with a different question, 'how can we maximize well-being?', you have to study folk who are already feeling amazing, find out why, and copy whatever the heck they're doing.

It's unlikely that marriage psychology has ever studied couples who are deliriously content or addiction psychologists studied people who aren't addicted, or child psychologists studied kids who are flourishing, or geropsychologists studied octogenarians who have a twinkle in their eye.

Those studies don't exist because, of course, the people aren't ill.

So rather than studying folk with ailments and inventing disorders to label them and remedies to cure them, wouldn't it be ace to study people who are already feeling amazing. Their zestful vigour and smiley faces mean they've been shunned by the psychology profession. I chose to study those who don't need curing because, let's face it, they might actually have the cure!

For 12 whole years. Longer in fact. The PhD took 12 years but the studying continues, stretching ahead like a meadow of spring lambs. In fact I turned it into an actual job and became a scientist of it. Yes, an actual scientist of happiness. A doctor of joy. The exact opposite of a normal doctor. I'm an *un*-doctor. An *un*-therapist. A happy-ologist.

Here's your ultra-quick win. Having sought out and stalked happy folk for a dozen years, the penny-dropper had happened within the first three weeks. I realized that my happy interviewees had exactly the same shit in their lives that I do! It rains on them too. They get caught in traffic jams. They also need a second mortgage to be able to afford a train ticket to London.

It became very clear very quickly that happiness was less about what was going on around you and more about your internal processing of those events. Yes dear reader, your ultra-quick win is to understand that happiness is an inside job.

Happiness is not an ex-perience, it's an *in*-sperience. That's basically it!

And this section is about egg-zactly that.

Get yourself comfy, here's the science bit …

The Transformers ('Science in Disguise')

The diagram below is my entire PhD distilled into one diagram. Over-simplified, obviously. If you want the full 12-year academically obfuscated 120,000-word version, it's downloadable from my website. Help yourself. It's designed to confuse and nonplus. Even hardcore insomniacs will be snoring by page 5. It's the hoop-jumping version I was duty-bound to produce if I wanted to become an 'expert'.

The real wisdom comes in the translated version, the uncluttered, plain simple English unveiling of the academic hieroglyphics. This is the burlesque dancer version, layers removed to the point of there being nothing to hide behind except lashings of common sense.

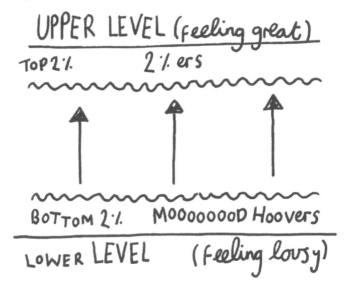

This is how it works. If, this week, you kept a diary of your emotions and we plotted the results on a graph, you'd have an upper and lower level. So, in a normal week, you will live your life between these two limits of upper level 'feel good' and lower level 'feel lousy'.

You already knew that.

The problem is that far too many people are spending far too much of their time in the bottom third of the diagram. Just to be crystal clear, I'm NOT talking about depression. Agreed, that's reached epidemic proportions and if you're having to take pills to get through the day then my heart goes out to you. Depression is when you fall below the lower-level level, when feeling a bit gloomy would be an upgrade. Clinical depression is a massive dip in energy, mojo, hope, purpose, and, often, loss of the will to live.[4]

The bottom third of the diagram? They are not that. They are just a bit stuck in huffing and puffing their way through life. It's low-level exhaustion often brought on by the manic pace of modernity. It feels like you've done a bout of British Bulldog (under-30s, Google it) where you're 'it'. Life delivers some over-the-top hurly-burly to the point where you feel like you've had a right kicking.

You can get stuck in the bottom third of the diagram. I call them mood hoovers or dementors. They suck all the energy

---

[4] *If you're currently below the bottom of the graph, this book might help but you're better off combining it with professional help. Seriously.*

out of you, leaving you feeling as rubbish as they do. The best two definitions of how to spot a mood hoover are: 'he doesn't have ulcers, but he's a carrier' and 'if there are two people talking and one looks bored, it's the other one'.

This is anecdotal, rather than evidenced, but I'd say it's those who complain the most who accomplish the least.

> 'Some people find fault like there is a reward for it.'
>
> *Zig Ziglar*

My academic interest has been piqued by the top 2%ers, my pet name for the small but perfectly formed collection of happiness outliers, the non-ill, flourishing few. Instead of the cold academic shoulder, I gave the zestful minority a welcoming embrace. Statistically they're oddballs who don't need counselling or to lie on a couch and relate tales of woe. It's important to note that they will have experienced plenty of woe, but the 2%ers are solution-focused, energetic, and can-do. They tend to get things done (while the mood hoovers roll their eyes and moan that it can't be done) and, crucially, they raise the levels of optimism and energy in those around them. In short, they're good to have around – at work and at home.

Most folk are trusting enough to take what I'm saying, understand that I'm simplifying it, and take the message in good faith. Like you'd want from a stethoscoped doctor. 'Spare me the jargon and give it to me straight doc.'

For the purists, the phrase '2%ers' doesn't appear in the PhD, it's my shorthand name for the positive few, their name chosen to signify their rarity value.

For the real geeks, I sifted my 2%ers through three data collections; they had to rate themselves as 8 or higher on a 1–10 happiness scale, they also needed to score in the upper quartile of the tried and tested Oxford Happiness Questionnaire and their name had to appear three times or more on a workplace survey that asked, 'who in your workplace makes you feel great?'

That last question is the wheat from chaff bit. This sorting hat corralled the self-nominated happy brigade into something subtler which I call flourishing. Flourishing is when your happiness leaks out of you and creates a feel-food factor in those around you. You're noticed, for all the right reasons.

It's the opposite of paranoia. Pronoia is when people are speaking nicely about you behind your back. Essentially, it's that handful of people who you can think of in your life who, when they're around, make you feel good too. Leakage. Emotional spillage. Upward spirals of emotion. This is the effect I was looking for.

I appreciate that academic purists will be able to pick holes in my methodology but if you go with the flow, these three hoops were pretty tricky to jump through. Remember, to arouse my academic interest you had to jump *through all three*:

  i. You rate yourself as happier than average;
 ii. You rate in the top quarter of a tried and tested academic happiness survey; AND

iii. At least three other people have named you as a person who creates a feelgood factor at work

Then, while the rest of the psychological community continued to scratch around in the darkest recesses of human misery, I looked at the sunlit uplands. The 2%ers are happier on a long-term basis and at a statistically significant level. Ditto their energy – they tend to report feelings of aliveness, vitality, and zest.

The problem with 2%ers? The clue's in the name. There aren't enough of them!

Activity: Who's who?

Who are your 2%ers? How do you know?

_____

_____

Who are your mood hoovers? How do you know?

_____

_____

The 'how do you know?' bit of the activity is crucial. You know your 2%ers are 2%ers because YOU feel great when they're around. Their upbeat emotional tone creates elevated positive emotions in you. And vice versa for the mood hoovers – they suck all the energy out of you leaving you feeling lethargic and drained.

The 2% stuff is an instant hit. A quick win. A breakthrough of the bleedin' obvious that gets you to step up your game, as of right now.

Keeping in the game – maintaining your new found 2%er status – that's the hard part.

This next bit is a slow burner. Don't expect results overnight. Yes, it's possible that things will fall into place very quickly but this is more like a six-month drip drip 'realization effect'.

Mental strength is like physical strength. If you want to get in shape you need to put some effort in. That six-pack stomach is there, but some bastard's gone and hidden it under 4 inches of Victoria sponge. Oh, and guess what? That someone was you! Lift some weights, pedal some miles, crunch some sit-ups, burp some burpees, press some press-ups. You can't just go to the gym once and think, 'that's me sorted'. It's a daily effort. Probably a grind in the early days.

Sucker punch number 1: you're not going to see the results for six months or so.

Sucker punch number 2: despite your best gym bunny efforts, that's only 50% of the deal.

The other half of physical fitness is about giving things up and, oh my gosh dear reader, I'm here to tell you that this is the really hard part. You need to stop eating Vic sponge, cut your drinking … and that bag of crisps in your meal deal – that actually turns it into a bad deal. The key to physical idolatry status is to do lots of good things and *stop doing bad things*.

Guess what? That's how mental fitness works too. It's easy to learn new ways of thinking but really hard to give up old ones. You've spent 40 years carefully grooving them in!

Before I do the solutions a quick word of warning. Please note, I'm not talking about bouncing around with jazz hands or moonwalking into the office declaring: 'Woo-Hoo, look at me everybody, I'm a 2%er!'. Remember, a 2%er is someone who makes others feel good, not someone you want to punch on the nose.

This is crucial. It means there's a degree of emotional intelligence involved here. Judging the mood and getting your positivity just right is a very inexact science. Too much and you'll come across as fake, jazz-handsy, or village idioty.

Think of your mission as one of being happy for the right reasons in the right place with the right people and by the right amount in order to raise the emotional tone of those around you.

One of the most difficult aspects of emotional contagion is getting it right.

I'm a Brit. I'm grounded in the real world. I don't do happy-clappy. I'm talking about you being your best self – *consistently* – because why on earth would anyone settle for anything less than being the best they can be?

But tens of millions do.

The 2%er Olympics

Here's an alternative way of looking at it. The Olympics. Once every four years the best in the world gather somewhere exotic to take on the best in the world.

THE LITTLE BOOK OF BEING BRILLIANT

It's great entertainment but because they're all superb we lose perspective. We know Mr Fast is fast and that he'll beat all the other 'not-quite-so-fasts' by 0.03 of a second. And chucking the javelin 80 metres is a long way. As is hop-skip-jumping 8 metres.

Ditto the Winter Olympics. Shooting headfirst down an icy hill on a baking tray – in less than a minute. It's bonkers and brilliant at the same time.

But I've got an idea to improve what is already the best show on earth …

We, the TV viewers, need to appreciate just how good these athletes are. So our recommendation is that in every competition, there should be an ordinary man or woman.

Let's call them 'Norman' and 'Norma'.

The Norms have been selected because they're totally average. Please take a moment to picture Norman … cheap suit, slight belly, slumped shoulders, exhausted eyes, hairy back, likes a trip to the pub, works in an office, eats pizza, has dandruff and that overworked haggard look about him.

And Norma? Same but an even hairier back.

The Norms have got their work cut out because they're going to have to compete in every single Olympic event. So, as Mr Fast and all those other not-quite-so-fasts stretch their chests at the finish line, Norm is rising from the blocks. As Mrs Swim stretches her exhausted fingers towards the end of the 100 m butterfly, Norma is adjusting her goggles and easing down the ladder into the shallow end. As Mr 10-Metre Springboard completes a triple somersault and lands without a splash, Norm bombs it, soaking the spectators. As Mrs Javelin nails a 65-metre throw, Norma mistimes hers, accidentally spearing one of the judges. *Oops!*

NORMAN   NORMA

But there are serious points to my new Olympic rules.

First, it's easy to be one of the Norms. It takes no training or dedication to achieve averageness. Bog standard is indeed the standard.

And second, it's not about the Olympics or, indeed, Norman and Norma. It's about life, and you. If there was an Olympics for attitude, positivity, optimism, enthusiasm, passion, resilience, and happiness – would you be normal?

If so, I'd like you to raise your sights to gold medal standard.

Welcome to the world of the 2%ers where rising above average means you'll stand out for all the right reasons.

You will have twigged that you already are a 2%er. *Sometimes!* This book is about helping you be a new improved version of yourself on a more consistent basis.

Think back to the last time you had a brilliant day? A day when you felt like you could take on the world. Think about all the good feelings you had. Invincibility, happiness, joy, positivity, energy, passion … you were being a 2%er.

Activity: You on a good day …

Describe yourself on that day (i.e. tell a story of you at your best). What happened, how did you feel, how did those around you feel?

_____

_____

The truth is that we all visit these fantastic feelings on an ad hoc basis. But what if we could learn to feel like that more often? What if your good days were less dependent on what was happening *to* you and more dependent on what thoughts were happening *within* you?

What if we could learn some simple principles so that feeling great became a habit?

More good news. You can, and it's deadly simple. Although not actually very easy (that's another subtle but important point).

Back to the 2%ers diagram, the difference between you at the bottom and at the top of the emotional spectrum is a game-changer. It's beyond obvious. You already know that the 2% version of you will have happier days, your relationships will be stronger, life will be more fun, you'll smile more and the chances are, you'll live longer!

Let's prove it …

Activity: You who?

We're going to stick you in Dr Who's TARDIS and send you 20 years into the future. We want you to write two accounts of your life:

Firstly, imagine that you've spent 20 years being one of the Norms. Everything's been hard work: work, relationships, weather, money. You've been a gold medal grumbler. 'Bog standard' has been your mantra. You've spent 20 years striving for mediocrity.

Stepping out into your future, please write an account of how life has turned out. For example, if you've had a negative attitude and bare-minimum work ethic for 20 years, what kind of job are you doing? What's your lifestyle? Where do you live? Who are you with? What kind of house, car, phone, etc? What do people say about you?

My life, age xx, as a mood hoover …

_____

_____

Second, I want you to write another future, this time having stepped out of the TARDIS as a 2%er. That's 20 years of positivity, growth, and go-getting attitude. Imagine, the best version of you for 20 years. So, same questions as above, write about your future:

My life, age xx, as a 2%er …

_____

_____

This book is peppered with dirty little truths, and here's a particularly hard-hitting one: not everyone fulfils their potential. In fact, most people waste it, living a black and white version of what could have been a technicolour, high-definition, surround-sound 3D epic.

Both of those futures can be yours. The question at this stage is, *how badly do you want the bright one?*

It's not worth pulling any punches. The biggest reason why most people are a million miles away from feeling brilliant, is that it's *easier* to be negative. Remember 'negativity bias' from earlier? It's how you're wired. You are a finely honed problem-spotting machine.

Yes, being yourself at your best requires effort. It's a learned behaviour. And because it's hard work and it takes practice, most people can't be bothered.

My message is *GET BOTHERED!* There's nothing more important that you'll ever do than create upward spirals of emotion. You'll feel better for it. And, crucially, those around you will respond in a positive manner. I'm promising that if you learn to be a 2%er and then do it for the next 40 years it will change your life. No kid gloves here. I'm not messing. I'm not talking about it having a marginal effect around the edges of your existence, I'm telling you that being a 2%er (and learning to stay there as often as possible) will fundamentally alter your life.

In egg-language, I'm not talking about decorating your egg, I'm talking about hatching. And helping others hatch.

Into a bright new world that's already there.

The Secret Sauce

Psssst. Wanna know the secret of happiness?

Come closer. Let me whisper (cue a furtive glance around to check nobody's within ear shot).

The secret's this …

There is NO fucking secret!

It's blinking obvious.

The data's in. The numbers crunched. The i's dotted. The Spearman's ranked. The T-tests calculated and bolstered by the Bonferroni correction. The scores on the doors have been added up and p-values are significant to $< .001$

We're good to go.

The findings are clear. There are several 'things' that 2%ers are doing that non-2%ers aren't. But those 'things' aren't actual 'things'. The differences in happiness are largely down to what I call 'intentional strategies', that is, habits of thinking and information processing that are common across the population of upbeat people.

To be clear, their mental habits are different.

To be doubly clear, they are doing some things that the rest of us aren't.

For triple clarity, they're also *not* doing some of the things that the rest of us are.

And if we're going quad clarity, all these 'things' that they're doing and not doing are obvious.

Their biggest intentional strategy is the simplest and most obvious. It's simply this: happy people choose to be positive. They actively and consciously choose an upbeat attitude. This is the single biggest strategy they deploy and, to be clear, just because you choose to have a positive attitude it doesn't mean the rain goes away, that bad drivers stop cutting you up, or that your imminent work restructure melts away.

The choice to be positive doesn't change anything in the external world. Rather it changes your internal world – your *thinking* – so you're better able to deal with the drizzle, commute, and restructure. Essentially, it's a mental upgrade that's in line with what Barbara Fredrickson calls 'broaden and build'. When you're feeling amazing your brain literally lights up, becomes more creative and can see possibilities and ways forward. When you're in 2% mode you're buzzing with ideas. You can see solutions. When your entire team is in 2% mode then the restructure is an opportunity. You become excited about the future rather than daunted by it.

Contrast that with the other end of the well-being spectrum. When you're in humdrum mode your brain is NOT in broaden and build territory. The same possibilities and solutions exist but you can't access them. Instead, your mind focuses on whatever problem is before you – the drizzle is grey, your fellow commuters are irritants, and the restructure means you're doomed. You can get stuck in this cycle of thinking and, to be blunt, rumination can lead to irritable bastard syndrome which, if left untackled, can cause some seriously dark days.

The choice to be positive is the single biggest thing the 2%ers do, so it's worth digging a little deeper. It falls into the category of common sense but not common practice.

And please note, I am not reporting that happy people choose to be happy. There are a lot of well-meaning syrupy Twittersphere memes claiming happiness to be a choice.

It's not. Happiness is an emotion. A feeling. You can open up to happiness and let it into your life a bit more, but that's 'allowing' not 'choosing'. Positivity, however, is not an emotion. It's an attitude. And attitudes are something you can take charge of.

Spookily, the better you get at consciously and deliberately choosing to have an upbeat attitude, the more likely you are to experience happiness.

My research also shows that actively choosing to be positive requires effort. It's much easier to coast through life on auto-pilot, putting effort into your emails and social media, but without ever really attending to the attitude you carry around with you.

I describe attitudinal choice like your eyelashes. Look around and what do you see? Look left. Right. Dart your eyes upwards and then downwards. Now left again, double quick.

Yes, the people on the train now think you're a weirdo as your eyes dart around at super-speed. You've taken in a lot of scenery but the one thing you haven't seen is your eyelashes. They're with you everywhere you look. They follow your gaze. And yet you never see them.

Choosing to be positive is similar. It's with you for every second of your life. It's with you when the alarm goes, while you're brushing your teeth and in the supermarket queue. It's even available in the dark moments, when your gran dies, when you lose your job, or you get trolled on social media – but most people aren't seeing it.

Same thing said better: only a small percentage of the population actively choose to be positive. In a sentence that didn't make the final cut for my thesis, the rest either don't know or can't be arsed.

To be blunt, why can you think of so many people who are getting by with a mediocre approach to life and so few folk who light you up? Because it's easier to do what everybody else is doing. To be a 2%er requires an awareness that an attitudinal choice is there for the taking but the double whammy is that *exercising* that choice can be hard work. Maintaining your effervescence, even more so.

I really do get that audiences are expecting something more complicated or academic-sounding than 'choose to have a positive attitude'.

Even some of those in my own team are on the sceptical bandwagon. *Is that it? You've been beavering away for 12 whole years and that's the best you can come up with. It's hardly 'new' information is it?*

Of course, the learning from my research is far more heavyweight than that. I'm not claiming that I've invented the concept of 'positive attitude'. I'm claiming the fact that, despite its apparent obviousness, only a tiny minority of people are exercising the choice. And, as a consequence, this tiny minority are living happier and more energetic lives. Oh, and their zest leaks out of them and creates an emotional updraft in those around them.

It's therefore worth reporting on some of the other facets that underpin their choice to be positive. As mentioned earlier, these fall into the 'things to start doing' and 'things to stop doing' categories, summarized in a handy at-a-glance cheat's guide to Dr Happy's results:

So he did. And they wouldn't.

After 12 years of psychological study, culminating in the highest level of qualification in existence, the psychological elders refused him entry. The doctor was puzzled. Like sturdy nightclub doormen the message was a very firm, 'sorry but we don't let your sort in'.

To his dismay, the doctor of happiness discovered that his strand of psychology isn't recognized by the doormen. He had perfected the wrong handshake. Perplexed, he visited the castle one evening, and being careful to avoid the crocodiles in the moat, he peered through a window. He spied a lot of old boys, bow-tied and cavorting in a cobwebbed library. The ninjas, it seems, are a very ancient club where tradition is valued much more highly than 'newfangled'.

Our hero was momentarily crestfallen. The old boys sure were revelling in their merriment. He figured that traditional psychology was about fixing broken people and medicating those that aren't fixable. Our doctor realized his schoolboy error; despite his advancing years he was in fact a new boy, not an old boy – he had failed to study phobias, disorders, depression, or irritable bastard syndrome, hence the door being slammed in his face and the drawbridge raised.

Rather than falling prey to chagrin and regret, this was the moment he realized just how much the seat of learning had taught him. The doctor had been pushing at the frontiers of psychology, pressing ahead into new territory that the olden times didn't know existed.

Peering through the castle window he realized he was outside the egg, looking in. The doctor had hatched.

He retreated silently from the castle, fearing the old boys might capture him and feed him to the crocodiles.

The doctor decided not to be bitter about being denied entry to the club. Instead of putting dog poo through their letter box, he decided to be proud to say that he *does not belong* to the Psychological Ninja Club. Even prouder that it's not his decision, it's theirs. He's barred. It means the doctor gets to quip a Groucho Marx line about his not ever wanting to join a club that would have him as a member.

The doctor knows that one day the club will modernize and he and the other hatchlings will be welcomed. For now, happiness, positivity, and human flourishing are subjects that remain outside of the egg, in a wonderfully sunlit corner of the otherwise dark, dank, psychological wilderness.

It's brighter here. There's plenty of sunshine. There are unicorns, rainbows, and flowers. People are smiling, workplaces performing, families flourishing, prisoners rehabilitated, and old folks dancing.

The place is buzzing with life.

This clearing is where the doctor spends his days, smiling mostly. He knows what he knows. He's been here for 12 years but can't help feeling there's lots more to learn.

Part 3

THE 3 Rs (RELATIONSHIPS, RELATIONSHIPS, AND RELATIONSHIPS)

Gosh, a love sandwich! This section is a warm love filling nestled between two slices of love.

In fact the word 'love' appears 36 times! It's mostly good clean wholesome love but, be warned, there's also some 18 certificate stuff involving your mum and dad having sex, as well as your gran and grandad (sorry about that image).

Moving on … Part 3 is a Barbie world. If you examine Ken, he doesn't have any manly bits, but he and Barb are different in other ways; emotionally for a start.

Then it's on to a whole host of 'home improvements', DIY positive psychology tips that will get your family in the zone. These quick wins are ancient and modern, ranging from Dale Carnegie's classic 'be genuinely interested' to the four-minute rule, growth mindset, and the little-known but rather epic Matthew Effect.

I also grapple with social media and argue that fortune (and, indeed, your children's futures) favours the brave.

There's some fun stuff but also tears (probably twice) before we move on to the workplace via Dolly 'part-timer' Parton and sea squirts.

For those familiar with 'Jimmy's Diary', you'll be delighted to know I've lifted it, word for word, and plonked it as a final rallying call that cements your home and work lives. If you've got no idea about Jimmy, adopt the brace position. There's an emotional ton of bricks about to fall …

You are shaping their world, but in order to shape it beautifully, you need to start with your own. And that's where the problems start! I can see how everyone else needs to improve – it's obvious!

But myself?

To be fair, on a personal level, most of us know what we need to do. That's the easy bit. But the 'doing it' bit? That's a different ball game. You've spent a lifetime crafting a version of you that fits in. Your egg, it's beautifully decorated and, quite frankly, nice and comfy.

And now you're asking me to change all that? To hatch?

The really short answer to that: yes I am.

If I take myself as an example: my first three and a half decades were perfectly fine. I had a steady job, lovely family, and all the trappings of the modern Western world (family car, central heating, four-slice toaster, enough food in my belly, a couple of warm holidays per year ...). Looking around, I matched up pretty well against my peer group.

And yet?

There was still something not quite right. If I dared take a closer look and ask deeper questions, it's safe to say I was an egg-dweller, a norm, a fair-to-middling, a 'mustn't grumble' whose life's purpose was only to remain within the accepted parameters of ordinariness. I was working incredibly hard but there was no escaping the fact that I had become a corporate drone, an acceptable husband, an okay son, a bog standard dad with a life like my middle-class lawn; mean, median, and mowed.

In order to be a more alive version of me, I had to up my game. For me that meant a cessation of drinking from the cup of bland and, instead, to start supping from the tankard of enthusiasm. Simple but crucial changes ensued – setting some huge goals, a rekindling of my learning, saying 'yes' more than I said 'no' and slowly but surely I began to chip away at the egg shell.

I learned that hatching takes time and effort. There's also a risk in creating a 'new improved' version of yourself – the risk being that your family and friends quite liked the old you. The more alive version of me? People might think I was bonkers, weird, or fake.

Remember, I've spent 12 years toiling for a PhD in Happiness. It'd be rather wasteful to write it up but not apply the principles to my own life. So rather than take a quick sip from the tankard of enthusiasm, I decided to drink deeply – *glug* – and accept the highs and the lows as a price worth paying for a life worth living.

That, dear reader, is the drinking game we're about to play. Tankards charged. I propose a toast: to you. Throw yourself at the eggshell walls. Chip away until there's a gap big enough to squeeze through. Step outside.

I'll drink to the superhero version of you that you've been hiding all these years.

To the superhero version of you. *Cheers!*

By the way, the liquor in that tankard is potent. Heady stuff. Elixir. It'll fuel you for this section of the book, in which we translate the science of wellbeing into positive actionable things to do, at work and at home. Think of it as rocket fuel for our lives.

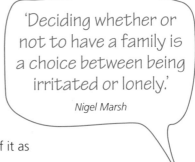

'Deciding whether or not to have a family is a choice between being irritated or lonely.'

Nigel Marsh

This next part is about home. Family stuff. Hence no swanky words or clever metaphors. It's got one ingredient; L. O. V. E. Love.

You can stop reading right now if you want. That's all there is. Page after page of the same top tip. Lashings and lashings of love. The Beatles were right, love is all you need.

If you want proof, as well as a few quick wins, carry on turning the pages …

Love is All You Need

Ignaz Semmelweis was a Hungarian medic, circa a lot of years ago, who had the bonkers idea that washing your hands before performing surgery would stop people dying.[2] Because, at the time (as recently as the mid-nineteenth century), the thinking was that people got ill from smells. So, if you had a fever, your mum would put a nice vase of fresh flowers in your room, to take away the stench and to make sure your smell didn't infect the family.

19th century thinking

Some flowers will make ya better!

[2] H. Wykticky and M. Skopec (2015) Ignaz Philipp Semmelweis, The Prophet of Bacteriology: https://doi.org/10.1017/S0195941700059762. Published online: 1 January 2015.

Around 1850, Ignaz's theory that these invisible germ thingies were killing people was, well, laughable. It's a sad story because they banged the poor bloke up in an asylum and, get this, he died of septicaemia at age 47, which, in a macabre twist of the ironic knife, could have been avoided if the doctors had just washed their hands.

Twitter hadn't been invented, otherwise I'm pretty sure Ignaz's deathbed Tweet would have been a simple #*FFS!*

Beliefs change. Olde-worlde thinking about bad smells was wafted away and new-worlde thinking about germs crept in. Doctors took it deadly seriously. They put huge effort into establishing antiseptic environments in children's hospital wards where, as a paediatrician in New York wrote in 1942, 'masked, hooded, and scrubbed nurses and physicians move about cautiously so as not to stir up bacteria. Visiting parents are strictly excluded, and the infants receive a minimum of handling by the staff.'

They also advised parents to minimize the amount of affection they gave to their children at home. Kissing, touching, hugging – all were ways to spread germs and therefore discouraged for the sake of the child's health.

Remember, this made sense at that time according to the knowledge they had.

Alongside germ warfare, behavioural psychology was coming on-stream, and academic psychologists began turning their attention to child-rearing. In 1928, John Watson, a former president of the American Psychological Association, published an important new book called *Psychological Care of Infant and Child* in which he warned against the 'dangers of too much mother love'. Showering a child with affection, he said, will spoil his character by breeding 'weaknesses, reserves, fears, cautions and inferiorities'.

The prevailing thinking was that hugging and kissing your children would spread germs, while letting them sit on your lap, holding hands, and all that bedtime story nonsense would make them weak of character. Too much love was a dangerous thing.

It's worth remembering that this was not a niche point of view. Watson was a best-selling author, the parenting expert of his time.

These super-hygienic, no hugging, 'speak when you're spoken to' environments were also applied to orphanages which, at that time, were legion. Remember, this was the 1920s. It was common for your mum and dad to have expired well before 30 or that they couldn't afford to feed you so you were wrapped in swaddling clothes and deposited on an orphanage doorstep.

Digging around in history, you find the orphanage mortality rate was close to 100%. Yes, you read that correctly. In some orphanages, almost every single child died before they were two years old.

It's too upsetting to paint a vivid scene, so I'll sketch it. Orphanages had established conditions of complete sterility and cleanliness. The tiles were scrubbed to shining. Each infant's bed was a safe distance from the next, and each crib covered with mosquito netting. Each baby was touched only when absolutely necessary, which is to say hardly ever. Nappy change, feed, and then back in your sterilized crib for 23 hours a day.

So, on the one hand, these children had the best possible start; a pristine environment, sufficient food, safe shelter, and as much protection from communicable diseases as possible.

But they were dying, en masse.

Enter René Spitz, a Nazi escapee who, in 1945, published the results of a seminal study on the critical role that love plays in the healthy development of a child. (I was picturing her as Nanny McPhee but Google has clarified that Spitz was indeed a man.)

Spitz compared two groups of disadvantaged children – infants who lived in an orphanage, and infants who attended a nursery at a prison in upstate New York. The children in the orphanage, all younger than three years old, were kept in a state of solitary confinement, the noble aim being to prevent the spread of germs.

Of the 88 children in the orphanage, where human contact was avoided, 23 had died by the end of his study whereas none of the children in the nursery had died. The finding exploded the idea that the children in the orphanages were dying simply because of exposure to germs. Rather, Spitz argued, they were dying from a lack of love, which compromised their health.

If you want to upset yourself, get along to YouTube and enter 'Grief: A Peril in Infancy' and you'll see a grainy black and white film of Spitz's work. It's the kind of experiment modern ethics no longer allows, a harrowing seven minutes that shows the decline of baby 'Jane' from a happy child to a blank-eyed wailing child. Her lack of human contact is as close to a child dying of a broken heart as you will ever see.

In fact I advise that you *don't* see it (I've got tears typing these words) and, instead, do the opposite. Love your children, even when they haven't earned it. Hold their little hand in yours. Read the best bedtime stories. Snuggle. Laugh. Be silly. Kiss. Rub noses. Build dens. Blow raspberries on their tummies, yes, even when they're 19.

In times when you haven't really got time, make some. It starts with kids but it's not just about kids. All the people in your life, young and old alike, need more than food and shelter to live full and healthy lives. They need love, hugs, and care.

Oodles and oodles of it.

Case proven, let's move onto the how bit …

A Potted History of You

I don't want to gross you out but in order for you to exist, your mum and dad must have had sex at least once. Hopefully, it was just a one-off, and you can now get the image out of your head. The gross bit is the number of sperm in a single shot which Google has just informed me, is about 500 million. And out of 500 million, you were the sperm that got to the egg first. *WooHoo!* You are already amazingly successful, the gold medallist sperm front-crawler. Or breast-stroker?

Or Man from Atlantis wriggler?

Whatever.

You burrowed into your mum's egg and, ping, you became a single-cell creature. Instead of being the 'potential to exist', you actually existed. The cells got busy multiplying and about nine months later you made a grand entrance into the blinding light of a birthing unit or, if you're like my niece, the reception area of Doncaster hospital.

Someone smacks your backside (nice welcome and first lesson learned!), you suck some air into your fledgling lungs, and begin absorbing the world around you. You have a certain genetic make-up but, other than that, you're a blank canvas, ready to be imprinted upon.

Your first day's a bit blurry. Hopefully you start to get into some sort of routine; eat, shit, sleep. That kind of thing. You might still be in a similar holding pattern?

Brains are much more active developmentally in childhood. Your first two years are characterized by crazy growth. By age two, you had over one hundred trillion brain synapses – double the number you have now. Yes, you bloomed at two! Your brain was alive with possibilities but figured it would never be able to use them all so from two onwards it stopped creating more connections and set about pruning the ones you already had.

So basically, at age two you could have been anything and anyone. Your brain was zinging with unlimited potential. From then on you started to become who you were going to be for the rest of life.

There was another massive spurt of development during adolescence, plus you grew some hairs and male or female bits and bobs. During your teenage years you experienced an overwhelming desire to be part of a gang, team, band, friendship group – your desire to fit in meant you started to dress the same as your chums. You had the same haircuts, listened to the same music, and watched the same things on TV. You thought you were super-cool but checking back through those photos, the truth is revealed!

Then from late teenage-hood your brain progressively solidified with your mature brain in place by your mid-20s.

Hopefully you get to enjoy some awesome decades of maximum brain capacity and then, without wanting to get too upsetting, the whole thing can go into decline. The wonders of medical science mean that our bodies can be kept alive beyond our brain's ability to stay in the game. The decline of your memory and personality can be heartbreaking. Enough said.

Let me be clear. Your early years were crucial. Your children's and grandchildren's early years *still are* critical!

In summary, brain growth occurs in such a way that it develops a stupid amount of axons, dendrites, and connections. Up until the age of about seven, you are a universe of possibilities. And, gradually, depending on your early years' experiences, these possibilities get narrowed down.

For me, there are two standout points here:

1. Although the rate of development slows, your brain never stops changing. It is a relentless shapeshifter, constantly rewriting its own circuitry.
2. The process of becoming who you are is less to do with what pathways grow in your brain and much more about what pathways get lopped off.

Bus Pass Barbie

Barbie's 60 and if a man is still allowed to pass comment on the looks of females, she's a bit plasticky, but is wearing her years pretty well.

Modern Barbie is worldly wise, saying things such as 'Get your sparkle on. Show this world where you belong' and 'Be a leader. Don't let anyone's actions influence you so much that you forget who you are.'

Go Barbie!

She's come a long way because one her stock phrases 60 years ago was 'Math class is tough'.

This political incorrectness has been deleted but if you'll allow me to continue in a mild politically incorrect vein, I'd like to point out that males and females are different.

I know! Imagine?

Males are endowed with physical strength. We were designed to chase and wrestle with warthogs, drag the carcass home, and, crucially, know which way was home. Females can do those things too, but with smaller warthogs, and the way home might be less clear. Sometimes left and right get confused.

But evolution has compensated by giving the female of the species a whole load of emotional superpowers. Generally speaking, females have less physical strength but a finely honed ability to 'tune in' to emotions as well as mastery of the dark art of understanding the meaning of what *hasn't* been said.

What the Lord gaveth the hog wrestler in strength, he tooketh away in emotional intelligence.

Sure, the modern world has loosened the roles a little but the point remains valid.

Deferring to Daniel Goleman[3] (the doyen of Emotional Intelligence), women and men differ in areas of self-awareness, managing our emotions, empathy, and social skill. We can pretend that males and females are the same, but they're actually not. There are many tests of emotional intelligence, with most showing that women tend to have an edge over men in this particular superpower.

The biggest difference between women and men is in the area of emotional empathy. If someone is upset, or the emotions are disturbing, women's brains tend to stay with those feelings. But men's brains do something else: they sense the feelings for a moment, then tune out of the emotions and switch to other brain areas that try to solve the problem that's creating the disturbance.

Therefore, women's complaint that men are tuned out emotionally is most probably true. But please bear in mind, it's not that we don't care, it's just that our brains are looking to seek a solution, rather than get mired in the emotion.

There are advantages to both. The male tune-out works well when there's a need to insulate yourself against distress so you can stay calm, keep a clear head, and make a rational decision. This partly explains why, according to the

---

[3] D. Goleman (1998) Working with Emotional Intelligence. New York: Bantam.

stereotype, men are calm, rational, and rarely swayed by emotion. In times gone by, this stolid patriarchal, 'wait till your father gets home' approach meant that the dad acted as disciplinarian. So, emotional detachment was the way things were. It's what men saw other men doing and the stereotype was passed down through the generations. Please note, I'm not trawling through history from the year dot – this is fairly recent stuff.

The female tendency to stay tuned in helps to nurture and support others in emotionally trying circumstances. It's part of the 'tend-and-befriend' response to stress.

The result of this emotional jiggery-pokery is that 35% of daughters say dads meet their emotional needs, as compared to 72% for mums.[4] Damn those bosomed humans with their emotional steroids.

So, if this was a school report, dads would find 'Must do better!' stamped on pretty much every page. In healthy family functioning, it's the fathers who deviate most from the norm. Let me say this as simply as I can: pretty much across the board, mums are superheroes. In the happiest families, it is the dad that also steps up to the plate.

Therefore, although this advice applies to both males and females, I'm aiming it more at males because they are the ones who need to pull their parenting socks up the most.

[4] J. Youniss and J. Smollar (1985) Adolescent Relations with Mothers, Fathers and Friends. University of Chicago Press.

119

For sharing, possibly pinning on the family corkboard:

10 things that require zero talent:

10 Things that require zero talent

1. Being on time
2. Work ETHIC
3. EFFORT
4. energy
5. body language ✔

6. PASSION
7. Doing extra ←
8. being prepared.
9. smiling
10. ATTITUDE

Emotional Soup and the Four-Minute Rule

Wouldn't it be a shame to have a wonderful life and not notice?

A lot of people do. Have a wonderful life, that is. And not notice. They grumble about their wonderful life instead.

Reflect back on first thing this morning. Did you rise and shine, or rise and whine?

Exactly!

The 'rise and whine' thing. It's a very easy habit to get into, hence why nearly everyone does. But you're not 'everyone'.

You're you. You're going to be extinct in the next 50 years. You're the last one of your kind left in the wild. You owe it to your species to be lively, interested, and positive.

It's worth noting that what you do every day matters more than what you do every once in a while.

Daniel Goleman talks about 'emotional soup', the concept that, in any social situation, everyone is adding a certain 'flavour' to the atmosphere, none more so than at home.

Two things spring to mind: first, dare to ask yourself what flavour you are adding to your family soup. Are you coming through the door with joy and enthusiasm or are you poisoning the family atmosphere with toxicity? And, second, not all family members are equal. Yes, everyone is adding something to the emotional soup but, as a parent, you are adding the most. For 'parent' read 'leader without a title' – your emotional contagion is massive.

For the record, I am not pontificating about you finding your impact or experimenting with it; I am screaming that you are already having it. This is a less than gentle reminder for you to wield your existing impact in a positive way.

Steve McDermott's four-minute rule is total genius.[5] Coming under the parenting heading of 'small change, big impact', it works because it's both. If we do away with the science of 'it is

---

[5] S. McDermott (2007) How to Be a Complete and Utter Failure in Life, Work and Everything: 44 1/2 steps to lasting underachievement. *Harlow: Pearson.*

a proven thing that you have data for?' and cut to the chase, it's this: it takes about four minutes for those around you to truly catch your emotional state.

Same thing said the other way around: you cannot NOT have an impact on other people.

How refreshing is that? Chill, in terms of the science from earlier, you haven't got to be a 2%er all day. Just the first four minutes will do. That's the first four minutes of coming into the office (happy, energetic, enthusiastic), going home, meal times, a business meeting – get the first four minutes right and everyone will have almost no choice but to catch your enthusiasm.

It's the smallest change that's had the biggest impact on my life.

In a bizarre tradition, many families go through a ritual of offloading all their emotional detritus on the ones they love most in life. Saving all your rubbish up to brag about seems like a strange thing to do but, nevertheless, it's very often what happens. I did it for years. If this habit occurs day after day, it has a cumulative effect on family well-being.

It's worth asking yourself have I had a bad day or just a bad five minutes that I've milked all day?

For me, the four-minute rule started with a question that I'd ask myself as I drove home from work – *how would the best dad in the world go through the door?* The answer was obvious, yet weirdly, I hadn't been doing it. So, that night, instead of coming through the door and going through the motions of 'How was school?

'Boooring.'

'What did you learn?'

'Can't remember.'

I decided that the change needed to start with me because, after all, it's not my kids' fault that their dad's asking such a shit question. One epic evening I came through the door and I nailed them with four minutes of being the best dad in the world. They were six and three at the time, so I pounced on them for some hugs and then asked, with genuine wide-eyed enthusiasm, 'How was your day? Was it good, fantastic or brilliant?'

And oh my gosh, what a different coming home experience I'd created. The kids picked out the highlights of their day (Ollie, age three, 'We had chips!') and their enthusiasm bubbled over though teatime, bath time, and all the way to bedtime. The first four minutes was like lighting a firework. All I had to do was step back and watch them sparkle.

So next day I did it again. And again. And again, until eventually it became grooved in as a family habit. We ended up shortening it from 'Good, fantastic, or brilliant?' to 'G, F, or B?'

And get this, eventually my kids ended up asking me about what was G, F, or B about my day at work. Look, I don't want to over-egg the point. Our household is not *The Waltons*. It's not hearty pumpkin pie and a cheery 'Night Jim-Bob' ringing out at lights out. I'm alluding to a small change in me that had a significant impact on my family. I got a chance to shape the 'coming home' experience, and I did.

Changing your wordage from 'how was your day?' to 'tell me about the highlight of your day?' is subtle. It's not a big change but, for me, it was a very big deal.

It became a habit. As with all the ideas in this chapter, it's the stickability that's crucial because in positive psychology practice makes *permanent!*

Added Interest

We've done 'new', 'borrowed', and 'blue' so it's about time I brought you some old, classic self-help advice from the 1930s. Harking back to Dale Carnegie's classic book, *How to Win Friends and Influence People*, his top tips are:

1. Be genuinely interested in the people around you.

   Obvious? Kind of.

   Easy to do as you're hurtling through life trying to get things ticked off your to-do list? Not very.

   Carnegie's wisdom is to be *genuinely* interested, not lip-service interested. And being genuinely interested in people takes time, effort, and a considerable amount of emotional energy. For instance, there's no point in bouncing through the door and asking your kids about the highlight of their day if, while they're telling you, you're scrolling through your emails.

And Mr Carnegie's other belter from the 1930s that still holds true today:

2. Say nice things about people behind their back.
    I'd maybe go a bit further and advocate that you say nice things about them to their face as well, but Carnegie's tip is a sure-fire winner on two levels. Firstly, if you say nice things about your family, friends, or work colleagues, it's likely that the grapevine will whisper it back to them. And how morale-boosting is it to hear that someone is saying nice things about you when you're not even there? Whoosh! The flames of a relationship are burning brightly.

    The second point is more technical. In psychology there is something that boffins call 'spontaneous trait transference' which basically means that if you are saying nice things about someone, the person to whom you're saying nice things attributes those qualities to you. This is all done at a subconscious level but I promise you that makes it more powerful rather than less.

    Carnegie hit on the fact that human transactions work in the exact opposite way to financial transactions. In banking you put rewards in and you get interest out whereas in relationships you put 'interest' in and you'll get rewards out. In fact the more 'interest' you put in, the more you'll get out.

    It's worth passing this information on to your children … have a guess what's the number one thing you can do to be popular at school? Is it to be drop dead gorgeous, or have a rich mum, or be a brain box? Nope. The number

125

THE LITTLE BOOK OF BEING BRILLIANT

one factor is to *like* people. The more people you genuinely like the more people will rate you as likeable.

Hence a weird sounding top tip to pass on to your kids is 'just *like* people'.

Praise Be

A child's readiness for school depends less on what they already know and more on whether they have figured out how to learn. Pam Schiller reports there are seven key ingredients, all linked to emotional intelligence: confidence, curiosity, intentionality (the wish and capacity to have an impact), self-control, relatedness, capacity to communicate, and cooperativeness.

That's a bit jargony so let me drop it into the real world. Teachers are reporting that, increasingly, children are coming to school unable to learn and, in some cases, unable to speak. To clarify, they're not mute. They *can* speak, but have heard so little conversation that they haven't learned.

It's a heartbreaker. At age four and a half these children can scroll, swipe, and click, but they can't write. They can grab a slice of pizza and stuff it in, but a knife and fork is alien.

'Most people do not listen with the intent to understand; they listen with the intent to reply.'

Stephen Covey

So speak. A lot. And listen, even more. But be *genuinely interested*, more than anything.

Child development fads come and go but one that's here to stay is Carol Dweck's 'growth mindset'. Sure, there's a steady stream of academics dissing her work (remember, that's what they do) but, for me, Dweck's conclusions are common sense. I'm less bothered about 'proof'.

Briefly, one of her experiments involved setting a group of children a really difficult exam after which one group was praised for intelligence ('You are sooo clever!') and the other for effort ('You've worked reaaally hard!').

Next, she did something rather harsh, setting a test that was impossible for them to complete and, guess what, the first group (praised for being clever) soon capitulated, figuring that they weren't clever enough. The second group (praised for effort) stuck at it and outperformed the others by 30%. Dweck's advice is that if your child accomplishes something, don't say, 'Well done, you are such a little genius!' But rather, 'Awesome, you put the effort in and got the reward.'

Applied to families, always praise effort rather than talent. If your daughter scores a goal at football, don't high-five her and say, 'Holy moly, total genius. You were born to play football.' According to Growth Mindset research (and common sense) you'd be better off saying, 'Amazing goal! That's what practice and hard work gets ya!' And ruffle her hair in a chummy fashion.

Or when your lad wins an award for writing stories? Rather than 'Crikey dude, you are destined to be the next Roald Dahl' try 'Amazing result mate, that's what you get for all those hours of hard work and for reading all those books.'

Let's take the example of reading – children who start off reading well will get better and better compared to their peers, because they will read even more broadly and quickly. The more words they learn the easier and more enjoyable reading becomes. On the other hand, it's very hard for poor readers to catch up because, for them, the spiral goes downwards. Thus the gap between those who read well and those who read poorly grows even bigger rather than smaller.

According to the Matthew Effect success snowballs, but so does failure.

Dads and grandads, I don't want you to think I'm having a pop at you but the biggest single factor in your son/grandson reading books is if he sees a male role model reading books. That, good sir, is YOU! (If you're a female reading this book, please find a male and read this page to them, starting with 'The Lord Giveth' and finishing with the next sentence …)

So even if you can't read, pretend!

The Matthew Effect shows up everywhere. Ben Zander talks about the transformation that happens when a young person learns to love music. For most, the early days are a chore. If you've ever suffered *Three Blind Mice* on a recorder, or caterwauling scales on the clarinet, you have my sympathy. The early days of learning a musical instrument are classic Eric Morecambe territory: 'they're hitting all the right notes but not necessarily in the right order'.

As a parent you have to hang in there and pretend you're enjoying it. Even then, some kids will quit.

But some ride through the storm. These kids lean forward and begin to play. They engage, either with the teacher or with the music. They achieve some early breakthroughs, maybe playing a piece that they recognize. As they connect they lift themselves off the piano seat, suddenly becoming what Zander calls 'one-buttock players'. They're lifted by passion and engagement. And from here on in, they experience giant leaps of learning.

If I'm allowed to stretch Zander's wonderful analogy beyond music and reading, if you want your children to find their passion (sport, maths, cooking, science, stand-up comedy; it doesn't matter what) the Matthew Effect says that some early wins are crucial in your child powering ahead.

The biggest thing you can do to facilitate that is to live it too. So, reading-wise, if the biggest thing a dad can do is to be *seen reading*, then it extends to all those other activities too. Put yourself out there. If you child is learning the violin, challenge yourself to learn it too. Play together. Paint together. Laugh together.

Trampolining. Bounce together.

Baking. Make cakes together.

Art. Draw together.

Stand-up comedy. Tell jokes together.

Science. Dissect frogs together. On reflection, that's messy. Go to the science museum together instead.

Football, kickabout together.

Spellings, learn them together.

Drama, go to the theatre together.

Join them. Add your buttock to their buttock. Live a one-buttock life together because two buttocks are better than one.

Following the buttock theme, you might need to sit down for this one. Oh, and there are no laughs at all. Quite the opposite in fact.

There's a saying: you only live once. And it's 100% wrong. You only *die* once. You live every single day. Admittedly, it can be a grind so you don't always feel like you're truly living, but 'aliveness' is a feeling that can be learned.

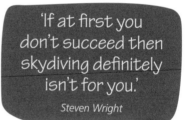

'If at first you don't succeed then skydiving definitely isn't for you.'
Steven Wright

Sometimes, the best way for people to wake up to the magnificence of being alive is to jolt them awake. Consider this next bit your defibrillator treatment.

Electrodes attached.

Clear?

Bzzzzt! …

Here's a true story, which makes it all the more compelling. A doctor decided to ask her patients what they enjoyed in life, and what gave it meaning. All well and good, except this doctor happened to work with terminally ill children. 'Terminal' is just the worst word. In an airport a terminal is where your journey ends and in a children's hospital, that journey is life. Their short journey is ending. They're not going to get to experience the pleasures of being an adult and their parents aren't going to enjoy the joys of parenting.

Gulp!

Here are some of the children's responses.

First: none said they wished they'd watched more TV, zero said they wished they'd spent more time on Facebook, zilch said they enjoyed fighting with others, and not one of them enjoyed hospital.

Interestingly, lots mentioned their pets and almost all mentioned their parents, often expressing worry or concern such as, 'I Hope mum will be OK. She seems sad', and 'Dad mustn't worry. He'll see me again one day in heaven maybe.'

Double gulp!

All of them loved ice cream. *Fact!* Also, they all loved books or being told stories, especially by their parents.

Many wished they had spent less time worrying about what others thought of them, and valued people who just treated them 'normally'. For example, 'My real friends didn't care when my hair fell out.'

Many of them loved swimming, and the beach. Almost all of them valued kindness above most other virtues: 'Jonno gave me half his sandwich when I didn't eat mine. That was nice,' and 'I like it when that kind nurse is here. She's gentle. She doesn't rush. And it hurts less.'

All of them loved people who made them laugh: 'The boy in the next bed farted! Hahaha!' (laughter relieves pain).

And finally, they ALL valued time with their family. Nothing was more important. 'Mum and dad are the best!' 'My sister always hugs me tight.' 'No one loves me like mummy loves me!'

Triple gulp!

Look here, dear reader, these are very big messages indeed. If you can't be bothered to listen to anything else in this book, then please listen to children who are arriving at the final destination of their very short lives.

If I'm allowed to summarize, it'd be something like this: Be kind. Read more bedtime stories (and read them like you want to), spend time with your family, crack jokes, lighten up, fart in bed, go to the beach, hug your kids. Love, love, and more love.

Eat ME!

Oh … and eat ice cream.

Often.

'Perhaps our eyes need to be washed by our tears once in a while so that we can see life with a clearer view again.'

Alex Tan

Anti-Social Media

For the record, I adore technology and the modern world. Ditto teachers, schools, kids, and education. The really good schools are places where imaginations really do run wild. It has very little to do with funding. It's about culture – a spine-tingling feeling you get when you walk through the door.

Sometimes that tingle is offset by a nagging feeling that we're stuck in an education system from a bygone era when Britannia ruled the waves. Mass education began in Victorian times when children were taught via chalkboards and school bells mimicked the factory bells that heralded a change of shift.

'In our offices and classrooms we have way too much compliance and way too little engagement. The former might get you through the day but only the latter will get you through the nights.'

Dan Pink

The chalkboards have been replaced with iPads and the bell is a buzzer, but the system is the same even though that rigid external world is gone.

135

THE LITTLE BOOK OF BEING BRILLIANT

The modern world craves novelty, creativity, resilience, and new ideas. This exists at age seven but is sometimes extinguished by 14.

Example? I gave a group of primary school children the task of rewriting the story of the *Three Little Pigs* from the wolf's perspective. It was truly heart-warming. Turns out he wasn't bad at all. Wolfie had endured a troubled upbringing, what with being born into a littler of nine, plus he had allergies to straw and wood. Suddenly, all that huffing and puffing makes perfect sense.

The same challenge to 14-year-olds and, guess what, they can't be arsed.

Young people go through a developmental stage whereby, for the first time, they begin to clock that other people have opinions of them. Add in their desire to fit into a social grouping and you get a heady dose of self-consciousness. The modern world has exacerbated the problem so whereas teenagers have always gone through a phase of being overly embarrassed, the modern world has added to their pressures. We've reached the point where 'not being bovvered' has an air of social coolness. It's the new black.

I can't do a chapter on 'positive grand/parenting/aunty/uncling' without addressing the biggest issue facing families today. Technology. Particularly social media and access to wifi.

There's a slew of published papers that are addressing these issues and I won't pretend to be an expert. However, if the biggest factor in well-being is 'relationships' then herein lies a splurge of my thinking and possible ways forward with regards to the contentious issue of family wifi.

I asked a lecture theatre of 15-year-olds what they do with their phone while they sleep. Nearly all slept with their phone, putting it under their pillow, on the mattress, or at the very least within arm's reach of the bed. They checked social media right before they went to sleep, and reached for their phone as soon as they woke up in the morning. Their phone was the last thing they saw before they went to sleep and the first thing they saw when they woke up. If they woke in the middle of the night, they often ended up looking at their phone. Some used the language of addiction. 'I know I shouldn't, but I just can't help it.'

It may be a comfort, but the smartphone is cutting into teens' sleep. Many now sleep less than seven hours most nights. Sleep experts say that teens should get about nine hours of sleep a night; a teen who is getting less than seven hours a night is significantly sleep deprived.

Adolescence is a key time for developing social skills; as teens spend less time with their friends face-to-face, they have fewer opportunities to practise them. What's at stake isn't just how kids experience adolescence. The constant presence of smartphones is likely to affect them well into adulthood.

In the next decade, we may see more adults who know just the right emoji for a situation, but not the right facial expression.

137

My generation has been the first to raise kids who are born into the age of mobile technology, and we are completely underqualified, having had no personal experience of what it is like to grow up with technology.

What do the experts say?

Well there aren't any! That's the whole point. The 'experts' in growing up as digital natives are currently age 11. The babes with iPads in arms.

I think there might be some simple ground rules gleaned from proper science as well as the tried and tested science of the bleedin' obvious. Note, with all household 'rules' they might be simple to introduce but they're not easy to enforce.

For example, I'm 99.9% sure that it's a great idea to delay technology use until your child reaches double figures. An iPad at age two or a smartphone at seven? Easy to do and, once you've done it, there's no putting the lid back onto Pandora's Box.

In the US there's a campaign called 'Wait until 8th', urging parents to pledge not to give their kids a smartphone until the 8th grade (or around 14 years of age). To me, it feels intuitively right. Imagine, if everyone in your community did the same, your children would know no different, skipping to school, chatting, flirting with proper eye-to-eye contact, focusing on their learning, making daisy chains, playing hopscotch at playtime …

But I have both feet planted in the real world. Getting your entire community to withhold smartphones until 14 is a romanticized ideal of the perfectly wholesome *Little House on the Prairie* school setting.

Recalling Deresiewicz's point about humans being the world's most excellent sheep, all the other parents have given their kids a smartphone for their seventh birthday, so you feel compelled to do the same. After all, it's only your old hand-me-down phone. It's only going to sit in the drawer with the other eight fossil phones. It's a rubbish phone but it'll make your child's day.

The pressure is immense.

Think again.

What you're basically saying in that scenario is 'All the other parents are lazy. It's rank bad parenting. I know it's the wrong thing to do and I'm robbing my kids of social intelligence by joining in with the smartphone thing but if the other parents are doing it, I have to do it as well.'

Read that sentence back to yourself.

And again.

Baaaaa.

Then stick to your fucking guns. You'll need fortitude and a big dose of pluck, so here are a few paragraphs to help.

Assuming you campaigned for 'Wait till 8th' you'd probably have dogshit smeared on your door handle from the group of bolshie parents who insist that their kid has a mobile phone

THE LITTLE BOOK OF BEING BRILLIANT

at age six in case there's an emergency. 'What if something happens to my little darling?' That brigade.

That's an easy one to rebuff. I'm old enough to cast my mind back to pre-mobile phone times. When something happened to you at school, what happened? Or if your mum desperately needed to get a message to you what did she do?

Do that. It worked.

Counter-intuitively, not only do children need to learn how to use technology appropriately, they also need to learn how to *not use* technology. I hear a lot of parents say, 'I had to get my son a smartphone because he has a 45-minute bus ride to school, and what else is he going to do?'

What, apart from stare out of the window, make eyes at the sexiest girl in the year above, chat with his buddies, tell jokes, give each other Chinese burns, or pick his nose and examine it really closely? If we teach our kids to turn to technology to fill every moment of boredom or discomfort, this strategy will stay with them their entire life. In doing so, we strip them of the opportunity to learn how to be alone with their thoughts, how to manage their own emotions, and how to be creative in figuring out what to do, or how to connect with those around them.

Technology is a great tool, and it's nice to have, but it always comes at some sacrifice. Sometimes, it's better to let kids be bored.

The bigger issue is this: will your child hate you for withholding technology? Yes, occasionally. But later in life when they can hold a conversation and make small talk, tune into the feelings in the room, and create strong and lasting relationships, they'll think that less screen time was great parenting. And because they'll have developed empathy and appreciation, one day they'll actually thank you.

My 99.9% certainty above tallies with your 0.1% hesitation that your child will get left behind in the rush to colonize cyberspace. I doubt that will happen. Technology is getting easier and more intuitive to use, so it's not as though kids need a 'head start' on figuring it out. Besides, all schools have iPads and classroom technology. Your kids will fly in these lessons.

Still not convinced? Here's the clincher: remember, catching up with tech is easy. Catching up socially is *impossible*.

Now to the really tricky bit!

In exactly the same way that a boy will be influenced to read by seeing his dad with his head in a book, your children will be influenced by *your* use of technology. If you're logged on, scrolling, swiping, texting, and emailing guess what your children will do?

And guess what you're *not* doing? While you're swiping, scrolling, and retweeting, you're NOT chatting or making eye contact.

It's hard to find clear guidelines for 'healthy' technology use. The platforms are changing so rapidly, we don't really know what is healthy. Here are The American Academy of Paediatrics guidelines, with a bit of my spice added:

Under 18 months	No screen time
18 to 24 months	Very limited time. High quality programming, with parents
2 to 5 years	1 hour per day (max). High quality programming, with parents
6 to 12 years	90 mins per day (max). Never after 8pm
13+	Negotiate reasonable weekly limit. At least one day media-free. Never at mealtimes. Never have tech in bedrooms. *Bed*-room, the clue's in the name
All ages	Never at mealtimes. Get a new fruit bowl that becomes a phone bowl. On entry into the house each phone goes into the bowl. That's where it'll be if you need it. Stand there, do your thing if you have to, replace it in the phone bowl, crack on with chatting

Parents	As little as possible when the kids are around. They are your priority and they need to know they're your priority

Other households will have more liberal access. Most will have no rules whatsoever. Yes, your teenager might grumble but that's what teenagers do. Relax, those next door with unfettered wifi access, and the ability to watch porn till 4am, will also be whingeing. It also transpires that they will be asleep in class the next day, they will be unable to sustain meaningful relationships when they're 25, and their sons, when age 40, will have watched so much porn that they're unable to get an erection in a normal loving relationship.

You are the parent. You're in charge. The climate in your house is your responsibility.

Do what's right, not what's easiest.

Thank you. From me, and also on behalf of your children and grandchildren 30 years hence.

Stop Faking It

If at first you don't succeed, congratulations, you're normal.

If you feel anxious, rejected, sad, or hurt, welcome to the human race. We all experience these feelings. They're what makes life so amazing. The trick is to not feel them too often.

We need to get comfortable with our kids not being okay. We need to allow them to feel sad, to realize that it's normal, and nothing to be afraid of. The solution to sad is most likely not to wallow on social media saying how sad you are, it's more likely a walk in the woods, a bike ride, or for dad to tell one of his rubbish jokes.

Ditto yourself. You too are allowed to have a bad day.

> 'I love you like a fat kid loves cake.'
>
> 50cent

Part 4 of this book is devoted to feelings, so no plot spoilers but a quick heads up; negative feelings – if you peek behind the magician's curtain, you'll see that it's not a whole lot of smoke and mirrors, it's just thought. If you're feeling anxious, it's because you're thinking about something that makes you feel anxious. Ditto rejected, sad, and hurt. Ditto happiness, joy, and pride. And every other feeling you've ever experienced.

I'm a serial bike-faller-offer. I've got a route, an off-road forest path that I delight in taking a bit faster than necessary. Most times, I'm off, but up and back on in a jiffy, scratched, bruised, and pride dented. Except the last time. That was a proper hurty fall off. It was dusk, I failed to see the fallen tree and next thing I knew I was in a bush, with my bike on top of me. As well as having a handlebar in my ear I also had a scratched back, bleeding knees, swollen ankle, mortified mojo. That kind of thing.

There was nothing to do except limp home and have a couple of steady non-cycling weeks. By some miracle, with no instruction from me, my wounds healed.

Your body is self-correcting and this is how your mind works too, but only if you let it …

There are times when life will be unspeakably dreadful. For those times, the solution is simple. It's called 'time'. It really does heal. It's okay to feel awful. In fact it's inevitable. It's part of being human.

However, there are far too many people feeling awful about the wrong things. There are a lot of things you can fake in life (*ahem!*) but the one we've mastered is the art of winding ourselves up and creating fake stress. Chasing someone across town because they've cut you up in the traffic, getting angry because there are teaspoons in the sink, shouting at the TV news, grumbling that your laptop has chosen this very moment to upgrade itself, these are examples of Vipasanna Vendetta, the magnification of tiny irritations into full blown anger.

We're the greatest of magicians, illusionists of reality, but instead of pulling rabbits from hats we're pulling big buck-toothed turds. Magicking shit out of nothing is, I have to say, quite a trick of the mind.

Examples abound. I was speaking at a conference yesterday and at break time the coffees hadn't arrived – cue total panic and arm flapping from the organizer along the lines of 'Oh my gosh, no coffee, this is my worst nightmare'.

To repeat, so it sinks in: *the late arrival of coffee is her worst nightmare*.

If your 'worst nightmare' is late coffee, you are living a charmed life. I'd suggest visiting war-torn Syria, being crammed aboard a refugee boat setting sail from Tripoli to Europe, or spending some time in a children's hospice.

The fact that you're reading this sentence means that you're richer and more educated than 99.5% of people in human history. Assuming that you're in the Western world, then you currently live in the most free and tolerant society that has ever existed. Your family may frustrate you, but over a third of the world's population has only one parent and 143 million children are growing up with no parents at all.

If you've been to university, you are part of the lucky 7% worldwide elite. You're unlikely to ever live at a subsistence level like almost 60% of the world's population and you surely won't ever be starving like almost 25% of the world population.

For decades, research has tied gratefulness and appreciation to happiness. People who are happier tend to be more grateful and appreciative for what they have. But it also works the other way around: consciously practising gratitude makes you happier. It makes you appreciate what you have and remain in the present moment.

If you write down ten things that you appreciate but take for granted, you'll be amazed at what crops up on your list. This isn't to say you must ignore what's wrong or broken with the world. I'm all for getting passionate and upset, but about the right things.

I'm one for going against the grain, so for those who say 'But surely Doc, a problem shared is a problem halved', I'd respectfully suggest that, no, you have in fact doubled it. To soothe the naysayers, I'm talking about letting go of the trivia, the 95% of your hand-flapping that comes from stressing about next to nothing. The habitual low-level *self-created* angst that puts you on edge all day every day. Big stuff, fine. Flap all you like. Get angry with the world if the world deserves it. But coming into the office tutting about the lack of car parking, or going through your front door chuntering about the traffic … let it go. Switch to the positives, if only for four minutes, and you'll feel better. The wonderful side effect is so will those closest to you.

Three years ago I ran a workshop for a newly formed group of deaf women in Derbyshire. Astonishing women, all of them. One young woman had a T-shirt emblazoned with 'Stay positive', which I thought was pretty cool. We did a selfie at the end and she confided that she didn't mind being deaf; it was her brain tumour that was causing her more grief.

Check out your list of ten and remember to shut up and be grateful.

147

Cease your pointless flapping and get a perspective.

By the way, in the conference example, the coffee arrived 45 seconds later.

Fun stuff

A) Teatime talks. Pick a subject and let the conversation flow ...

1. If you do what's easy, your life will be hard and if you do what's hard, your life will be easy. True or false? *Explain.*
2. People who live in comfort zones are actually extremely uncomfortable. *Discuss.*[7]
3. It's OK. It's always OK. Except when it's not and that's OK as well. *Waddayathink?*[8]
4. Go out looking for friends and you will find very few. Go out and be a friend and you will find many. *Really?*
5. Being lazy pays off now. Hard work pays off in the future. *Discuss.*
6. What 20 things would you like for Christmas? *That aren't things.*
7. Stop trying to be the best in the world and start trying to be the best FOR the world. *What the heck does that even mean?*[9]
8. Mondays are being bullied. Everyone hates them. *What are we going to do to stand up for Mondays?*
9. There are no mistakes, only lessons. *Bunkum, or true?*
10. The best thing about the person to my left is ...

---

[7] *Borrowed from D. Taylor (2016)* How To Be Successful By Being Yourself: The Surprising Truth About Turning Fear and Doubt into Confidence and Success. *London: John Murray Learning.*
[8] *Ibid.*
[9] *Thank you, Gavin Oattes.*

B) More fun stuff ...

Here's some fun-for-all-the-family homework. Try it with your six-year-old. Take a trip to your local graveyard and have a wander. For the absolute best educational experience it's best done on the stroke of midnight, in a thunderstorm, so the lightning briefly illuminates the tombstones.

It's a bonding experience. It's actually quite sweet. Your child will be gripping your hand ever so tightly.

Wander amongst the graves. It's the perfect time to explain about death. And the undead.

Take a torch. As you're meandering, have a read of the tombstones. Ask your six-year-old to read a few out and through chattering teeth, sobbing and *'I wanna go home to mommmmmy'* they'll read engraved statements like 'Here lies Horace Whiplash. Father, husband, brother. Sadly missed'.

And 'Mabel M. Boniface. Dearest wife and mother. Loved and loving.'

Challenge them to find one that says 'Here lies Dave. And he was really cool because he had a Lamborghini', or 'Dear departed Mary. She was epic cos she was minted' or 'In memory of our dearest mother, Kylie, who will be remembered forevs for her really epic selfies and she had so many pairs of shoes it was like totally unreal.'

When you think the point's been hammered, return home for several sleepless nights.

Snuggle Up

The Danish concept of hygge (pronounced 'hoo-gah') has gained traction in the UK, largely because of the Danes' lofty world happiness league position. While the Brits languish at number 19, Denmark consistently ranks in the top three happiest nations on the planet, taking the coveted #1 slot for eight years on the bounce. They are to world happiness what Bryan Adams' *Everything I Do* is to chart topping.

So, interest piqued, let's have a look at Danish culture. The images we see tend to be filtered through the lens of interiors magazines, which represent hygge as a soft take on Scandi home design – with unlimited tea lights, a cosy throw draped over a sofa, and a brimming mug of hot choc.

Hygge is all of those things but, as I've discovered, it's also a whole lot more. Indeed, it's less about stylish living and more about living better; at home, at work, and within a community.

So what the heck is it?

Hygge is more than just a word. It's a concept that also has equivalencies in Sweden (Mysa: to be engaged in a pleasant or comfortable activity; to be content or comfortable; to get cosy; to snuggle up) and Norway (Peiskos: fireplace cosiness, sitting in front of a crackling fireplace enjoying the warmth).

Danish hygge is about cosiness, warmth, and being enveloped in snuggliness.

Hygge is more than a word, it's a philosophy. I love hygge because it's primitive and basic and, even better, you can't buy the right atmosphere and sense of togetherness. Neither can you hurry it.

Hygge starts with three principles: pleasure, presence, and participation. It's often associated with eating or drinking, but the more it counteracts consumption, the more hygge it becomes. In fact, the more money and prestige is associated with something, the less hygge it is! How wonderful is that? Drinking tea is more hygge than drinking champers. Playing board games is more hygge than playing computer games. Hygge is easier to obtain in Blackpool than Mauritius. Home-cooked cake is more hygge than bought.

In Denmark you can hyggesnak (hygge-chat) in the corner shop; enjoy hyggeaften (a hygge evening) with chums, and wish your children 'Hygdig!' (have Hygge) as they come home from school.

There's an element of mindfulness in hygge; the idea that we are engaged in the present.

'Hygge is uncomplicated noticing; joie de vivre,' says Thomsen Brits. 'We enter wholeheartedly into the moment and taste all that it has to offer.' Your winter porridge, your autumnal walk, sitting on a British beach freezing your bits off, fresh coffee (from your favourite mug), Sunday brunch, cottage pie, fresh flowers in a vase, snuggling up and sharing a box of Maltesers …

151

Hygge is a brief moment of pause, solace from the craziness, the smallest of moments that make a big difference to how we live, feel, and interact.

If it works for the happiest country on the planet, it'll work for me. And if I can do it, so can you. Hygge is a wonderfully simple concept to introduce at home. Become hygge spotters.

Turns out that almost the same thing exists much closer to home, in Wales. *Cwtch*, to get cosy. To hug/cuddle; a sanctuary; a safe, welcoming place.

Hygge, Mysa, Peiskos, Cwtch … shout out your moments and amplify the snuggliness and love. It works for me.

The Squirts

And so to business … briefly, because it's a big deal but not as important as home stuff.

Fact – the humble sea squirt paddles around until it finds a rock, attaches itself, gets comfy, and then eats its own brain. Its brain is useful in finding something to attach to but, once that bit's done, it doesn't need to think any more so it scoffs it, thus providing a bit of sustenance so it can hang on for the rest of its dear life.

I think there might be a human equivalent, people who have settled on their rock, being bombarded against the tide, and who stay put. Even though there might be a better rock, a bit higher where the sun makes life more pleasant and the waves are less intense. But, metaphorically, they've eaten their own brains.

Some businesses have also eaten their own brains.

There's a very good chance that staff numbers have been butchered to the point that there is no slack in the system, everyone is at full throttle and 'feeling amazing at work' is something the old ones remember, misty eyed, from back in 1983. Those 'good old days' when we used to go to the pub at lunchtime …

> 'I hate my supervisor. Behind her desk it says, 'You don't have to be mad to work here, but it helps.' 'Mind you, she's written it in her own shit.'
>
> *Alan Carr*

Dolly Parton was lucky, she only worked 9 to 5. Nowadays, that classes Dolly as a part timer. She was also keen that you pour yourself a cup of ambition, so here's a brief tour through how to shine at work. Obviously, all the previous points about family still hold true for the workplace: four-minute rule, say nice things about people behind their back, praise effort rather than talent and suchlike.

First of all, context. Businesses are mad keen on measuring stuff. Schools do it, hospitals do it, your boss does it. The birds and bees probably do it too, who knows?

So we set up complex systems to record customer feedback, or exam results, or numbers of hip operations per week. The lady on the supermarket checkout is monitored by the speed with which she bleeps your items through. And we measure these things because they tell us how efficient we're being. These measurements give data, which we can look at, which will help us do things faster and better. We don't half like a hefty wedge of 'big data'.

But it's my belief that most of the most important things in a business can't really be measured. Try measuring creativity, excitement, commitment, buzz, happiness, confidence, team spirit, or love. I'd argue that, in business, it's the things that can't be counted that really count.

There's plenty of evidence that employee engagement is positively related to well-being, attendance, profit, staff turnover, customer satisfaction, shareholder return, business growth, and success. All heady stuff. So why is it that only 18% of employees are actually engaged in their work?

Of course, it's easier to feel great if you're doing a job you love. Whether you're engaged in your work depends on whether you view it as a job, a career, or a calling.

If you're doing a 'job', you'll feel it in the pit of your stomach. Going to work will be a chore. You're doing it because it pays the bills and you get that feeling of angst when the alarm goes off at stupid o'clock.

A 'career' is a necessity but you see opportunities for success and advancement. It's up the evolutionary scale from a 'job' and you're likely to feel you're moving in the right direction. You're invested in your work and want to do well.

A 'calling' is where the work is the end in itself. You feel fulfilled and have a sense of contribution to the greater good. Work is likely to draw on your personal strengths and gives your life meaning and purpose. And, whisper it quietly, you'd probably do it for free.

Whether you're engaged in a job, career, or calling has less to do with your work than you might imagine. A calling orientation can have just as much to do with your mindset as it does with the actual work being done. Please let me remind you of the modern-day classic; a man was sweeping the floor at NASA and when someone asked him what his job was, he replied, 'I'm helping put a man on the moon.'

Turning a janitor's job into a 'calling' is very powerful indeed, both for the individual and the organization.

Business leaders have attempted it by doing what the consultants have been telling them, working stupidly hard to create an environment where employees can feel satisfied at work. Indeed, for a hundred years or so 'job satisfaction' has been what we've been aiming at.

But is it the bullseye or just bullshit?

155

Just for a sentence or two, let's unpick 'satisfaction'. What does it actually mean? If you come back from holiday and report that it was 'satisfactory', what are you really saying? Or a satisfactory meal out. Or, dare I say, that post-coital warm glow when your lover asks 'how was it for you?' and you puff on your cigar and pronounce it to have been 'satisfactory'.

Satisfactory is a low bar. I've just synonymed 'satisfactory' and this is what I got: adequate, all right, acceptable, sufficient, passable, quite good, average, competent, not bad …

So for a hundred years we've been aiming to create organizations in which people feel fair-to-middling.

Employee satisfaction's all well and good if you're striving for mediocrity.

Recently we've seen the rise and rise of engagement, a much higher workplace bar, connoted by absorption, immersion, enthrallment, and captivation. This sense of engrossment stimulates a state of higher energy. Being enraptured at work is akin to the psychological state of flow, when time flies and you're being challenged in just the way you like to be challenged. You are uber-productive, super-creative, and you feel energized rather than depleted.

This is your organization's competitive advantage because your customers catch it too. After dealing with your team, your customers are going home and talking about their experience. In the modern world they will be sharing it online, a mass of raving fans driving customers to your door.

I'm delighted to say that engagement is what I've been studying. I've been up to my welly-tops, trudging through workplaces, picking out the best of the best. In no way am I looking to diminish the superb work that many organizations have already done. There are a lot of mouth-watering, open-plan, coffee-machined, pool-tabled workplaces where leaders have truly empowered their employees to take control of their days and think for themselves.

And yet even in these jaw-dropping environments there are still employees who fail to engage. I worked with a superb organization, I'd say the best of the best, and the boss was rolling his eyes because someone was complaining about the wrong kind of free Coke in the free fridge in the free kitchen next to the free table tennis table and the free comfy seats. Apparently 'diet' and 'original' are okay, but 'zero' is his drink of choice.

This links to a deeper rooted workplace problem, that employee *engagement*, the feeling of aliveness, zest, and vigour, is in the head of each individual employee. A workplace that's been carefully crafted to be better than home is amazing, and worthwhile, but it's only half the engagement story.

Engagement, you see, is partly an internal construct.

The Leadership Multiplier Effect

The quickest route to employee engagement is via a rethinking of leadership. And in case you think you're not in a leadership position, you are. Robin Sharma nails it with his concept of LWT, leading without a title.

The quickest route to employee engagement is via a rethinking of leadership.

In my work with organizations I keep coming up against the same questions:

- How can we motivate our people (and keep them motivated)?
- How can we change the culture?
- How can we make our customers go 'wow'?
- How can we get people to take responsibility?
- How can we get staff to change?
- How can we improve teamwork?
- How can we break down silos?
- How can we engender trust and build a no-blame culture?

And I've noticed that they're all about how we can change other people. This typifies how normal organizations approach management: the person in charge learns how to manipulate the thinking and behaviours of those in their teams. So we go round in circles of manipulation.

Leadership courses are about things you can do to get other people to cooperate and/or work harder. All the courses you've ever been on are additive.

I'm coming from the other end of the spectrum, the subtractive 'what do we need to stop doing?' end; the number 1 leadership point being STOP GETTING IN THE WAY OF YOUR PEOPLE!

There's a term I came across in my research – 'entropy' – which is basically a law of physics that was originally about machines. In simple terms it states that any machine, if left alone, will lose energy. It just seeps away. Therefore new energy has to be applied. Entropy is this 'new energy'.

The simplest example is a family experience from 1974. My dad went out and purchased a brand new Austin Maxi, green with vinyl roof. If you're under 40, it's worth Googling. The Maxi, along with its sister car, the square-steering-wheeled Allegro (I swear this is true) were so bad that they actually signalled the end of British motor manufacturing.

In those days you had to run an engine in for the first 5000 miles, which meant, in practical terms, you were restricted to a maximum of 40 mph. I remember a family holiday to Cornwall that involved a three-day drive to get there, a quick pasty on the beach, and three days home.

I digress.

My dad never managed to sell his existing Vauxhall Viva. He put a couple of ads in the *Derby Evening Telegraph* but, alas, no takers stepped forth. The Viva sat on our drive all winter, unused, rusting, losing its lustre. It started out red and gradually turned pinky orange. The tyres went flat. It even developed a dent in its bumper, all of its own accord (looking back, I wonder whether it was self-harming?) My dad's Viva was the principle of entropy in action. It wasn't going anywhere. Its energy just seeped away. It became more and more knackered.

In the end the scrap man gave my dad a fiver and towed it away. It will have had a happy ending, acting as a donor, providing body parts for other cars who needed a transplant.

Entropy also applies to people and organizations. 'Corporate entropy' is when organizations and teams run out of energy. Literally.

Check out the following list, warning signs that energy is leaking away:

- There is no longer time for celebration.
- Problem-makers outnumber problem-solvers.
- Politics. Having to fight against the system.
- Back biting and low-level grumbling about other teams and other departments.
- Teams 'over-communicate' and 'under-converse' (you email the person sitting next to you, and copy 85 people in to cover your backside).
- The pressures of day-to-day operations push aside our concern for vision and creativity.
- Too many people have that 'here we go again' feeling.

- People speak of customers as impositions on their time rather than opportunities to serve.
- The focus is on getting through the week. Surviving rather than thriving.
- Celebrating the end of the week with 'dress down Friday' or doughnuts or a cheeky early finish.
- Staff come alive at 5.

Tick the ones you're guilty of. All are energy leakages which can be plugged by mixing with staff who have a spring in their step. That comes from purpose, as well as mixing with other staff who have a spring in their step.

Kim Cameron's work on organizational vitality examines four types of energy: physical, mental, psychological, and relational. The first three are depleted throughout the day. Physical energy is diminished by calorie burning, psychological energy by mental concentration, and emotional energy is sapped by long meetings.

But the last one, relational, is renewable. In contrast to the other three, relational energy increases as it is exercised. Cameron describes relational energy as uplifting, invigorating, and rejuvenating, concluding it to be 'life-giving rather than life-depleting' (p. 51).

And where does 'relational energy' come from? People, that's where.

And we come full circle. Cutting to the chase, physical, psychological, and emotional energy are depleted during the day. The only way to renew your energy is to mix with 2%ers. Putting bright, optimistic, smiley people in key communication nodes – that's an obvious quick win.

Yet businesses are not doing it!

This week, it was my fifth trip to a wonderful organization and, having learned from trips 1 to 4, I already knew what to expect. For some reason they have chosen the most miserable person in the entire organization and given her the job of receptionist.

No matter how great you feel as you stride across the car park to sign in, you will feel suicidal by the time you've got your badge. I've had five visits and tried five different tactics; I've bounced in, smiled my way in, bantered in, consoled my way in, and frowned back. Nothing. Not a glimmer of the merest hint of upturned lips.

And of course, it's not just visitors. Every single member of staff who comes through those revolving doors must feel like revolving right back out again. They're met by a rusting Vauxhall Viva, right there on reception, with moss growing on the inside of her windows. It's serious organizational energy leakage.

I'm not having a go at this lady. I'm sure she's a perfectly warm human being who loves her family and does some nice things for her church. She's symptomatic of the system; wrong person for that particular job. I would imagine that she cracks a smile at 5pm on a Friday but sticking her on reception is both unfair on her and unfair on the staff.

Put a 2%er into that role and you'd achieve a rapid change in culture. It's beyond obvious. And yet it's not been done. Equally importantly, find that lady a job that plays to her strengths (smiling isn't one, but she will have something tucked away somewhere, 'champion milk curdler' maybe?) and she'll come alive.

To be clear, I'm *not* advocating a no-holds-barred, gung-ho cadre of unwarranted positivity. There's an art to standing out. You can stand out for being a jerk, or a bully, the office gossip, or the arse licker. I'm not talking about any of that nonsense. Remember, jazz hands and *zip-a-dee-doo-dahing* your way into the office on a drizzly November morning is 'village idiot' category.

My 2%ers have been percolated through the filter paper of being nominated as 'who in your workplace makes you feel great?' I dare you to ask yourself, honestly, whether your name would crop up on that list. And I mean asking with brutal honestly. No kidding yourself.

If your name would crop up, this chapter's been a reminder to keep doing whatever it is you're doing.

If not, those socks? You need some garters.

Jimmy's Diary

To round off this family/business section, here's a story that I used to kick off the original *Art of Being Brilliant* book. No apologies for the repeat. No explanation required. It still gets me.

Here it is, word for word …

He hadn't been up there for years. Probably decades! In the faint light of the attic, the old man shuffled across to a pile of boxes that lay near one of the cobwebbed windows. Brushing aside the dust, he began to lift out one old photo album after another.

His search began with the fond recollection of the love of his life – long gone. He knew that somewhere in these albums was the photo he was looking for. It was the black and white one, when she had that smile. Patiently opening the long lost treasures he was soon lost in a sea of memories. The old man wiped away one or two happy tears. Although the world had not stopped spinning when his wife left it, the past was more alive than his present emptiness.

Setting aside one of the dusty albums, he pulled from the box what appeared to be a diary from his son's childhood. He couldn't recall ever having seen it before – or even the fact that his son had kept a diary. Opening the yellowed pages, he glanced over the entries and his lips turned up at the corners in an unconscious smile. His eyes shone and he chuckled aloud. He realized he wasn't just reading the words … he could hear them, spoken by his young son who'd grown up far too fast in this very house. In the utter silence of the attic, the earnest words of a six-year-old worked their magic and the old man was carried back to a time almost forgotten. The spidery handwriting reflected on important issues for a six-year-old – school, football, holidays, arguments with his big sister – entry after entry stirred a sentimental hunger in the old man's heart. But it was accompanied by a painful memory that his son's simple recollections of those days didn't tally with his own. The old man's wrinkles became more deeply etched.

He remembered that he'd kept a business diary. He closed his son's journal and turned to leave, having forgotten the cherished photo that had triggered his initial search. Hunched over to keep from bumping his head on the beams, the old man stepped down the wooden stairway to his office. He wasn't sure what creaked most, the stairs or his knees!

He opened a glass cabinet door, reached in and sought his business diary. He placed the journals side by side. His was leather bound, his name embossed in gold. His son's was tatty and frayed with a hand-drawn picture on the front. The old man ran a bony finger across the name 'Jimmy' scribbled on the cover.

He opened his business journal and read some of the entries. There were notes from meetings, often very detailed. Every single day was crammed with business appointments. Sometimes the evenings too. He remembered back to those times … he sure was driven in his career. It was for the love of his family that he'd chased success so hard.

The old man was drawn to an entry much shorter than the rest. In his own neat handwriting were these words, '*Wasted a whole day fishing with Jimmy. Didn't catch a thing!*'

With a deep sigh and a shaking hand he took Jimmy's journal and found the boy's entry for the same day, June 4th. Large scrawling letters pressed deep into the paper read, '*Went fishing with my dad. Best day of my life.*'

Part 4

WHAT NEXT FOR HOMO SAPIENS?

Personal development

Taking you to the very TOP ↑

Like every other author, I'm vulnerable to 'kleptomnesia' – accidentally remembering the ideas of others as your own. So here we are. Me and thee, at Part 4 of the trilogy, playing out a gag that Douglas Adams originated and I'm borrowing.

There is plenty of original thought in this book but, admittedly, some of the ideas have been lifted. Bizarrely, some of them are borrowed off me. Can you steal from yourself? Anyhow, I have. From an earlier version of me who was full of enthusiasm but didn't know what he knows now.

The whole book has been breadcrumbs, designed to lure you this far. Part 4, the bonus section, is for the hard core, the self-helpers who really want to help themselves. This is where the breadcrumbs stop and you become the opposite of Micky Flanagan. Stick with Part 4; read, re-read, absorb, do, and you'll be *in* in.

Parts 1 to 3 have been the Billy Joel of personal development, the most non-threatening, easiest of reading. Things are about to turn ugly. Someone's taking the piano man outside to mess with his fingers and make sure he never tinkles those ivories again. While he sips soup through a straw, it's time for a gender change, an uptown *girl*, Sophie Ellis-Bextor.

'Murder on the dancefloor.'

It's about to get messy. Whack the music up.

Let's boogie …

Part 4 is brought to you by the word **Erschlossenheit**. German / n. / ɛɐˈʃlɔsn.haɪt / err-*schloss*-un-hite. World disclosure; the process by which things become intelligible and meaningfully relevant to human beings.

Mindless Non-Violence

Warning: this chapter is seriously challenging. Pass me a needle and a camel because I reckon it's easier for me to thread a double humped mammal through the eye of that bastard needle than it is for me to fully grasp the content of what's about to come your way.

The question is, of course, why? Why do I feel the need to up the ante and take you from the sunlit lush greenery of personal development to the harsh and windswept snow-capped peaks? Why not just keep it simple? Why risk alienating my readership with altitude sickness?

Three reasons.

Firstly, if I can get you to the top of the personal development mountain, the scenery is incredible. The world looks different and oh so wonderful. Hence I'd like to share the view.

Second, goats. Mountain goats live at the top (you're going to meet Jean Paul in a page or two. This will make sense then. Maybe?)

And third, this section takes me to the edges of what I know. I adore positive psychology and I love disguising my PhD and presenting it with a dollop of fun, but to embed the messages, you need more. This part of the book is me hand-holding you to the summit. If you come with me, it'll give the themes of this book some stickability.

But remember, Part 4 is what my wife warned me against (her exact motivational words were: 'Whatever's in your head, write it down and we'll publish it when you're dead. I don't want people thinking you're a dick while you're alive.')

Consoling myself with the thought that Van Gogh's wife probably thought his sunflowers were shit, I'm about to introduce you to a broad coalition of concepts around spirituality, consciousness, reality, mindfulness, and what a previous version of me might have labelled 'new age hokum'.

So let's start gently and a little left field, with Britain's favourite snack. Crisps. All crisps are just crisps – plain and simple sliced and fried spuds. Then they stick them in a vat of flavour and the sliced potatoes take on the identity of smoky bacon, roast chicken, pickled onion, squirrel, or whatever.

Same with you. You started out as just plain and simple you. Then we stuck you in a big vat called 'life' and flavours stuck to you. You might be 'generally upbeat but with a bad case of the Mondays' or 'a proper grumbler' or 'kind and loving', 'self-centred', 'confident and go-getting', 'a little bit poisonous' or, indeed, 'squirrel'. (I agree, that last one doesn't make much sense, which is exactly why I fought with my publisher to keep it.)

Jacki Huba says it better with 'we're born naked and the rest is all drag'.

The point being that it's not long into your 4000-week journey that you develop an ego; your flavour, the person you *think*

171

you are, the story you tell yourself, your preferences and hates. I'm coming back to this later but for now remember 'ego'; it's your identity, the version of you that you create in your head.

Newborn babies don't have an ego. They have what's called the 'original face'. A baby isn't trying to be anything or anyone, it's a human being rather than a human doing. When you paddle yourself through that birth canal into the bright lights, you have no idea whether you're white, brown, black, Jewish, Muslim, Hindu, Jedi, or whether you're destined to support Derby County, Arsenal, Partick Thistle, or none of them. You've no idea whether you're going to be someone who lives an abundant life, or someone who plays it so cautiously that they miss out. You haven't decided whether you're a confident or non-confident person, whether you'll take illegal drugs or eat too much cake on a regular basis.

You're not born with prejudice or religious intolerance.

All of the above are learned behaviours, choices that we make according to the upbringing we have.

Let me paraphrase a newspaper story that gives a heart-warming example of how we all start out …

your 'original face'

In recent times there's been a security crackdown. So airports have become more onerous, often requiring you to step into a glass chamber, legs splayed, arms aloft, as they take some sort of naked picture of you. We don't question it. We do as they ask, hanging onto the glimmer of positivity that the naked picture shows your back passage is clear of heroin and as degrading as the system is, it's more humane than the alternative rubber glove treatment.

This heightened security has spread to concerts and public gatherings. There's a wonderful story about Kai, a four-year-old boy who was new to all this. A keen WWF wrestling fan, his dad took him to a big venue where fans were routinely frisked on entry. All of them, even the four-year-olds! The boy wandered through the metal detector, the red light picking out the £2 spending money buried in his pocket. The security guard knelt down to the boy's level and opened his arms, showing the four-year-old what was required. The lad, assuming the best, opened his arms and went in for the full hug.

And that was where the newspaper story ended. Whether security went on to discover a flick knife tucked into the lad's belt, or a kilo of hash in his socks, who knows?

I'd say it's unlikely because Kai is how we all start out, primed for love, not hate.

Guru Guff

Next stop, oh my goodness, Eckhart Tolle. What. Can. I. Say?

Hold tight for this one. Tolle's argument is that the universe is consciousness trying to escape into the daylight. Hence, from the first spark of universal energy, consciousness has been looking for a way to be aware of itself. Consciousness's bid for freedom has taken billions of years to get to the point of being at the cusp of something approaching success.

Hence, consciousness is rising. Consciousness is becoming conscious.

You can loosen the grip of the sides of your chair. Chill. You're not supposed to understand it. Tolle's a guru. He's capable of having thoughts that nobody else has. He might be right. If I could understand his writing, I'd be able to have an opinion.

But I can't, so I haven't.

I'll tell it exactly how a guru doesn't.

If he's on to something, it's probably this: looking back through history there have been many revolutions – Bronze Age, Enlightenment, Industrial, French, Russian, Velvet, technological, medical, educational, Arab Spring, nano-technological, cyber, quantum – where big things were a-brewing or in the case of quantum, the smallest of things are the biggest of deals.

Nose to the prevailing wind, I can sniff the whiff of consciousness. The next revolution, it's blowing this way. There might be a hint of what some might call 'spirituality', a non-Godly scent of feeling connected. Or, sniff again and it might just be bullshit?

The whiff of bullshit

Who knows?

So I guess the first stop on the Number 4 bus tour must be consciousness; what the heck is it?

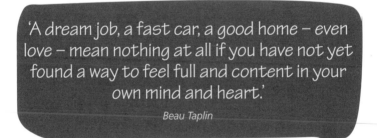

'A dream job, a fast car, a good home – even love – mean nothing at all if you have not yet found a way to feel full and content in your own mind and heart.'

Beau Taplin

I've really sweated over this next bit because to make my case, I first need to pick a fight with meditation and nobody EVER goes fisticuffs with the most popular self-help strategy of all time. No sane author is going to be stupid enough to challenge the mystics, take Buddha head on and leave him shaking his chubby fist at you. Why would you risk alienating your readers, the mindfulness crowd, and open the door to 1-star Amazon reviews?

175

I'm wedged between a rock and a hard place. What you gonna do Andy, tell the truth and ruin your entire career, or bottle it?

Fingers crossed that fortune really does favour the brave. I'm going truth and dare.

I'll start by kleptomnesiacking one of the stories in Russell Brand's deliciously honest and forthright book on addiction.

'To steal ideas from one person is plagiarism. To steal from many is research.'

Various

Not all perfumes are vegetarian. There's a certain type of goat, a musk goat, that earned its name by stinking of sheer, unadulterated gorgeousness. For the purposes of this story let's work with one of the flock, called, for argument's sake, Jean Paul Goatier. Jean Paul is highly prized by the perfume trade because a few squirts from his musk gland escalates the price of channel water to Eau de Chanel. The musk gland is connected to Jean Paul's balls, hence it's only the boy goats that are intoxicating. These glands are worth £45k on the black market because the smell is rumoured to be an aphrodisiac. At £45k a pop, John Paul and his flock are ripe for crossbowing.

Of course the goats don't know any of this. John Paul has no idea that he smells like a posh lady's boudoir. But taking a crossbow bolt to your flank and then having your balls squeezed of their juice, it's no wonder these billy goats are gruff.

176

Anyway, John Paul and his clan, they trip-trap around the foothills of the Himalayas, eating moss and dodging arrows, getting their Chanel fur snagged on thistles and trees. The goats then smell the fragrance and are entranced, wondering where the smell came from. Jean Paul Goatier spends his entire life in lovelorn pursuit of the heavenly smell when, in reality, all he actually had to do was stick his nostrils up close to his own gonads.

There's a message in their somewhere. Lads, it's not quite as literal as you may think? Unless you're double jointed, you're never going to get down there. I think the message is more ethereal, along the lines of 'the search is over. Look within.'

But of course, this 'look within' message is hardly new. Aristotle and his mates were pontificating about it way back.

Henry David Thoreau referred to this when he wrote that most people 'lead lives of quiet desperation'. We paper over the cracks of meaningless in various ways; we seek solace in buying things, shoes especially. Or we throw ourselves headlong into work, or a relationship, or we escalate to dampening the numbness with fishing or collecting train numbers or imbibing substances. Maybe we can medicate away our emptiness? Or drink our way out. Or eat, shag, and pray our way out.

> I asked the Doctor whether masturbation causes poor eyesight.
>
> He said, 'You're in Sainsbury's, mate!'

Hence the rise and rise of the oldest happiness trick in a very ancient well-being book, meditation, the turning of the mind away from the objective content of experience towards where it came from in the first place.

Meditation is both simple and deep at the same time. The aim is to catch yourself being the source of your thinking. It's the awareness of being aware. Quieten the shouting between your lugholes and you'll discover, fleetingly, that you are the creator and experiencer of said thoughts.

The clever meditative retort is that if, like me, you haven't got time to sit around pondering nothingness, that's when you really need to take time out to do exactly that!

I'm not pouring cold water on the most popular happiness remedy on the planet. The meditation bandwagon is huge, in full swing, and gathering no moss. I'm not saying meditation doesn't work. If it does it for you, then keep doing it. It's a technique to quieten your mind down and that's my whole point, right there; it's a *technique*. Something you have to do.

I'm more interested in NOT doing. An *un-technique*.

I once worked with a guy who meditated, earnestly, for up to two hours a day. He was a meditation anorak who would bore me about Transcendental, Qi-Gong, Zen, and Body Scan. I once went round to his house when he was *omming* and noticed he got angry with his kids while meditating. That's a big fat clue that it's not really working.

That's why I want to introduce you to Syd Banks' three principles of mind, thought, and consciousness, sometimes called innate or inside-out thinking. It's a proper *un-*technique. Syd's three principles are about the very nature of thought. In a nutshell, if after meditation, you keep getting angry with your kids that's because you think your kids are making you angry.

Beditation: Meditation for teenagers

Hence, this fundamental shift to the inside-out nature of thought. Your kids aren't making you angry. The way you're *thinking* about your kids – that's what's making you angry.

That subtle shift of emphasis is inside-out's magic sauce. It's a paradoxical mix of the smallest thing that's the biggest of deals.

I'm parking Syd for a while. We'll collect him later.

Meantime, I'm fairly sure this failure to live in the moment is a uniquely human problem. It's that pesky neocortex again, the bit above your eyebrows. The bit that zebras don't have, and neither do cats. Take my mog as an example. She doesn't laze around pondering the meaning of life. To clarify, she actually does laze around (a lot) sitting on her cushion, paws tucked underneath, eyes closed, perfectly feline in every way. Zen Cat. I doubt she's anywhere near achieving the upper levels of Maslow's fabled hierarchy. My puss ain't self-actualizing. Neither is she fretting about life's responsibilities or wondering whether she should shop around for her car insurance renewal

179

or just go with last year's company. Yes, yes, I know the quote's gone up by £40 but does that £40 offset the hour of my life that it's going to take to log on, trawl a price comparison website, and get the paperwork swapped over?

She's not wondering what other cats think of her, whether her flea collar is last year's look, or whether her bum looks big in the mirror. My puss is posted on Instagram (by my daughter) but isn't posting on Instagram. I'm not sure she even has an account. Indeed, I've shown her a video of herself, 'Lookie here Bubba, at my sleek all-you-can-eat-data iPhone that costs the same per month as feeding a mid-sized African town, remember this from last Christmas? This is a vid of you climbing the Christmas tree and pulling all the decorations down. I tweeted it and got 35 likes', and she seems totally disinterested.

She feigns disinterest to the point that she won't even look at the screen. How come cats have taken over the entire internet when they can't even be arsed to show enthusiasm for the output they star in?

It's almost as though my Bubba can't comprehend the meaning of 'self' or to understand time, consciousness, social media, the juxtaposition of my overconsumption while poverty abounds in Africa. It's not dawned on my pusskins to question why her adopted family puts up a pretend fir tree in reverence to a 2000-year-old tale of the Virgin Mary's firstborn that none of them actually believes in.

None of this has crossed her feline mind.

Because it can't. She hasn't got the mental software.

And I think to myself, lucky puss.

Tell Me About Yourself ...

If you've ever faced the classic lazy interviewer question; 'Tell me about yourself?' where did you start?

Let me guess, the likelihood is that you pitched in at a high level; where you live, current job, family, your interests, etcetera.

You didn't begin at the actual beginning; 'Me? Well, I originated as a zygote, a single-cell explosion of my dad's sperm with my mum's egg. *Boom!* Yes siree, that's how I started out. Then I pretty much kept doubling in size, swimming in amniotic fluid for six weeks. Then there was an injection of hormones that turned me into a male of the species. You see, up until six weeks, I was a human template. I had the potential to be female until six weeks. To be fair, we all did. In my case, it was testosterone, so I got some dangly bits. But I also got nipples. Which is weird, cos I doubt I'm ever going to need them.'

You didn't watch the interviewer's brow furrow as you ploughed on enthusiastically: 'Then, you'll never guess, after nine months the most amazing thing happened. I came out of this tiny tunnel into the fresh air. Woah! The shock of it made me cry. I'm a bit embarrassed by the next year or so. I shat my pants a lot. But, wait, it gets worse, I spent six months hanging off my mum's tits.

181

Nowadays, I've mostly grown out of those habits. I'm made of 27 trillion cells, each with an identical genetic structure and I'm married to someone the same, but with more oestrogen that's allowed her to have nipples that actually work …'

> 'When I was younger I felt like a man trapped inside a woman's body. Then I was born.'
>
> *Yianni*

If you want the job you learn that 'tell me about yourself' means name, rank, and serial number rather than molecular structure. You reel off a story of who you think you are, not what you actually are.

What you *actually* are is matter that's learned to be aware of matter – a cellular structure that has evolved with the gift of thought and the power of consciousness. Your biology is driven by feelings. Indeed, everything you do you do for a feeling.

We're not driven by logic and/or big words. When I earn money, I don't want money, I want the feeling of security that comes with it. And when I spend it on a nice shirt, I don't want another shirt, I want the feeling of super sexiness when I wear it. And when I eat cake, I don't really want cake. I want a feeling of comfort that comes with said slice of lemon drizzle.

So, if everything you do you're doing for a feeling, it's worth exploring the root cause of feelings.

Where the heck do they come from?

When my daughter was little she had lots of cuddly toys and she loved them all. But Sophie reserved extra love for a pink cuddly rabbity thing that she dragged around with her during the day and tucked up beside her at night.

Kids are supposed to be whizz bang creative, right? The name of the pink rabbit thing? *Pinky!* That's the creativity myth, exploded right there.

Anyhow, Pinky was a bit grubby but she didn't care because that pink rabbit made her feel amazing. He brought comfort, safety, and familiarity. If I was to ask my little girl about Pinky she'd swear that the feelings were coming from the rabbit. Pinky was making her feel all loved up when, of course, the feelings were totally coming from *within* my little girl.

Thankfully, I didn't know all this way back then because I'm not sure how I would have explained it to my six-year-old. Stroking her hair of an evening and consoling her sobbing as I explain that Pinky is actually nothing more than a piece of pink cloth, with beads as eyes and stitching for a nose, stuffed with cheap foam, assembled by Xin Ping, a 36-year-old mother of one (she had others but they were aborted because of local rules at that time) working in a sweat shop on the outskirts of Guangzhou.

Somehow, the truth is less romantic.

My point is that as adults, we're doing exactly the same. We've moved on from Pinky but we've attached our emotions to grown-up things. We are hook, line, and sinkered into thinking our feelings are coming to us from football results, a new car, your partner, work, a big gas bill, your kids, your special pants, or as was the case in the previous chapter, your apartment in Spain. Whereas the truth is (of course!) that feelings are always generated from within us.

Not 99.9% generated from within 99.9% of the time.

100% generated from within.

100% of the time.

This is where it gets tricky because, although you know this to be true, the world is very good at making you think the total opposite. Just as my little girl would have sworn blind that Pinky was making her feel safe, you will swear double blind that your feelings are coming from the outside. And if you think that, you will spend your entire life getting upset about things that are happening *to* you.

Your partner's upsetting you, you're cussing at the bad driver and chuntering to yourself in the supermarket queue. The soundtrack of your life is a gentle background noise of low-level grumbling. Sometimes the tutting boils over into rage. You're good at keeping it hidden, but it sometimes spills over into something visible; a sigh, shake of the head, a rant or middle finger salute. You become an angry person. If you don't know any different, that's how your life goes.

Please note, most people will play out their entire 4000 weeks thinking this is how life works.

If your anger persists, it morphs from a momentary feeling into a mood ('I've been feeling it for a while'). If that mood hangs around it becomes a temperament ('it's how I feel most of the time') and settles into a full-blown personality trait ('pissed off with life; it's just who I am').

This simmering discontentment is creeping down the age range. For young people nowadays it's less 'coming of age' and more 'coming of rage'. Here are some exams, and student debt or an unpaid internship and room to rent in a house you'll never be able to afford. The media loves to prod you with a stick and provoke some irritation, causing you to boo and hiss. There are a lot of angry people around who, if you stopped them and asked why they were angry, they've forgotten. It's just 'everything'.

If I'm blaming my partner or cursing my boss, I end up thinking about them – a lot. Guess how 'thinking about how rubbish your manager is' is going to make you feel? And venting about it to your partner at 6 o'clock every night, guess how that's making your partner feel? Your kids are listening in. In fact, they learn the ropes and, before long, they're sharing how pointless their day at school's been and you're embroiled in a nightly competition of 'who's had the shittiest day?'

Staying on the poo theme, if you've stepped in dog shit, you don't bag said turd, take it home, lay it out in your kitchen and re-enact stepping on it in front of your gagging family. 'I was walking along and there it was, and I stepped in it like this and it got stuck to my shoe and stunk to high heaven.'

185

THE LITTLE BOOK OF BEING BRILLIANT

You moonwalk across someone's lawn to clean the poop off and are careful not to step in it again.

Plus, and it's a subtle one, you don't get home and rejoice in all the turd-free pavement that you've walked on that day. You don't relate your walk from the station that was 'a gorgeous half mile of clean pavement'. Nope. You don't brag about that. You save the shitty bit to share with those you love the most.

Metaphorically, we're dwelling on the smelly stuff. The world out there is affecting me in here (picture me tapping my skull).

Before we move on please quieten the screaming in your head – the one that's shouting 'I get the general point but surely things are unequivocally bad, right? Why should I welcome the crap if it's my enemy?'

Relax, I'm coming to that …

The Rise of the Machine

Syd Banks' three principles shift us from an outside-in to an inside-out view of the world.

Everything's reversed. Instead of raging against the machine, Syd's insight was in realizing you *are* the fucking machine!

Just to be clear, Newton didn't discover gravity. It was already there. We're soaked in it. If a caveman kicked a pig's bladder into the air, it came back down again, in exactly the same way that a modern-day football does. It's just that Captain Caveman never thought it through.

In the same way, Syd Banks didn't invent his so-called three principles. To be fair to the canny Scot, he never claimed he did. They've always been there, hidden in the very best place, in plain sight. He didn't 'discover' them, he 'uncovered' them.

I never met Syd but he's modern enough to be on YouTube. I don't want to big him up too much but he's rather Messiah-like – beard, sandals, softly spoken, lots of followers, that kind of thing. I'm not sure he ever walked on water but he used to *work* on water, a welder in the Glasgow shipyards by trade.

Then, one day, he had one of those wakey-wakey moments that all reality is an illusion. That's a pretty big thought to have on a rainy Tuesday in Scotland. I'd say he had a riveting day in all senses of the word.

Syd's insight was around the three principles of mind, thought, and consciousness, so we need to unpick those. Briefly! (because too many books are written about the 3 Ps and an *entire* book ends up wrapping you in philosophical reef knots).

Your *mind*, it's the spark. It connects you to life, your own and other people's.

Your mind allows you to have *thoughts*, roughly 80,000 of them per day, a continuous stream, some good, some bad, some downright dangerous. The 80k are the ones you get as far as thinking – there are another million potential thoughts buffering, ready to step into your life if chosen.

Consciousness is the gift that allows you to experience thoughts. It's the animator that brings your thoughts to life. It attaches emotional special effects to make your thoughts real.

That's pretty much it! Syd spent the rest of his life sharing his insights, preaching his version of the gospel, the holy trinity being mind, thought, and consciousness.

In a nutshell, the argument is that thought creates your entire world. Always has. Always will. And you are the thinker.

Amen.

3 P.P.P. Principles

You are *feeling* your thinking. Gosh, that's such a big sentence, not in wordage but in philosophical tonnage.

It's a complete reversal of how life appears to you but it is, nevertheless, the way you operate.

Always!

You can never have a feeling without first having a thought. If you're anything like me, you'll have to let it settle for a wee while.

The secret sauce comes from the fact that the three principles aren't about doing anything. They just 'are'. If anything, they're about NOT doing.

But that kind of language is confusing, so let me reflect on the impact this has had on me. As I've become more immersed in *inside-out* thinking, outside influences have caused less of a stink. I'm a whole lot calmer.

Your boss will still be a dick, the bad drivers will still be bad drivers, the politicians will still be slimy, the weather inclement, and your kids will still leave pots on the top of the dishwasher instead of *inside* the dishwasher, but their power to upset you has gone.

You're free!

I worry a lot less. I feel clearer of mind because I have less on it! I feel less stress, less anger, and I have fewer arguments. I haven't had road rage for seven years (yes, I might have caused some, but I haven't physically chased anyone across town or felt the need to deliver a middle finger salute for a very long time. Not since the notorious 'Bangor-on-Dee Incident' of 2012.)

The weight of the world I'd been shouldering, that Atlas feeling, it's gone.

Life's not perfect and I sometimes forget but, overall, life feels lighter. As a result, I am enjoying it a whole lot more.

There will be naysayers reading this, those who are thinking, okay Dr Smart Arse, all you're doing is avoiding the issues.

189

What am I supposed to do, be gracious to the bad drivers, let my crappy boss get away with treating me badly, and let my offspring get away with not washing and tidying their pots?

No. Absolutely not. It's a lot more powerful than that. Inside-out thinking just lets them fall away. If I'm not feeding them, I'm not having anxiety and panic attacks. The bad drivers will always be there, as will the rubbish bosses, the long queues, and rainy days. The sink is still full of dirty mugs and skanky teaspoons but their power has been zapped.

And when the weight has gone, my thinking is clearer, and solutions start gushing. Best of all, my relationships are stronger. I've stopped trying to heal the world. The world is as it is. It always will be.

Look around. You'll see a lot of people waiting for the world to be perfect. Shouting at the injustice and unfairness. Ranting at the queues. Chuntering about fuel prices and young people nowadays.

As I've learned to cease trying to mould the world to fit what I want it to be, and accept it for how it is, I've found that I've accidentally fixed myself. I can have an opinion on politics, a strong one, but if I really want to change things I'm going to have to become

> 'If at first you don't succeed, try, try again. Then quit. No use being a damn fool about it.'
>
> W.C. Fields

a politician and create a political stir. And I can't be arsed to do that, so I'll vote, and chill. Other people can have the opposite opinion and that's fine. They can get angry. They can shout at the news. That's fine too. If they channel that anger into something productive, good on 'em. But if they just end up with an ulcer, then they've been pressing a self-destruct button.

If the rain wants to rain, it will. The rain doesn't give a flying fuck whether it's ruining my day. Me grumbling has no effect on the climate out there, but it sure affects my internal weather, the dark cloud outside mirrored by a low-level chuntering about a drizzly Monday.

It's not the rain folks. It's the way I'm thinking about the rain. Or, to go to the level of Syd Banks' three principles, it's merely an awareness that *I am the thinker*.

If you investigate Syd's books you'll see that his blinding flash of enlightenment was Buddhism, with a dash of Hinduism. He mixed in some Aristotle, Shakespeare, and positive psychology too I might add. He stirred it all up and left it in a pan to simmer. Syd's genius was that he accidentally left the brew on the heat for too long and all the froth bubbled away. He was left with the essence of personal development, the absolute distilled 100% proof good stuff. The truth that you can't distil any further.

Essentially, the remainder of this chapter is about that. The goo. Jean Paul Goatier's 'Essence of Well-being'.

For the perfect recipe, read on …

Living a Counterfeit Life

The content of your thought is less important than the realization that it is thought.

If we apply a smidge of science, it gets even deeper. The power of thought creates your current impression of the past and the future. If you're in a good mood, your past seems kind of okay. When you're in a foul mood not only is 'now' contaminated but everything you ever did is tainted with crapness too. 'Nothing ever works out for me …' and you get a gush of memories trawled up from the pit of misery. Your wonderful memories – the joys, loves, and successes – are conveniently hidden from your mind.

Also, the power of jumping aboard a positive thought right now also affects your view of the future. It's called Broaden and Build; when you feel amazing a whole load of future possibilities arise. Things seem doable and dreams achievable, so a happy now means you stride out towards a wonderful future.

At least, that's the theory. But, dear reader, life isn't some theoretical adventure that pans out all rosy. It's full-on and very rough and tumbly. As I outlined in Part 1, the pace

'Give the world the best you have and you'll get kicked in the teeth. Give the world the best you have anyway.'
Kent M. Keith

of life has picked up to the point that the normal rough and tumble can feel like a right good kicking.

Life is a serial offender, GBHing the shit out of good people.

I'm lucky enough to do a job I love and have just about enough freedom to do it how I want. Yes, I chat to clients about their needs and craft my workshops and keynotes to fit, but I also have flexibility to give my messages an 'Andy spin'.

With Syd's principles zinging in my head I started to go above my pay grade by introducing this information into my workshops. I wasn't ready. I love the 3 Ps but, by heck, they're slippery bastards. No matter how enthusiastic I am, you cannot mask doubt, even the merest hint of it leaks out to your audience.

My early audiences were sceptical. What about chemical imbalances, trauma caused by severe abuse in childhood, bullying, and post-traumatic stress disorder? The Nazis? Am I saying these are illusions? There were some jabby fingers pointed my way, from people who are suffering.

They were sharpening their pitchforks. 'Are you saying we made these things up?'

Gulp! This is the really hard part. A harsh fact of life: bad things do happen to good people. When the perpetrator committed the horrible action it was very real indeed. I'm in 100% agreement that the trauma was horrible when it happened. But now it's over. Or even if it's ongoing we still have the power of creation to make meaning of it for our lives.

193

What are we going to create: something to harbour and haunt ourselves with for the rest of our days, or something that was horrible then but from which we can rise stronger?

> 'I forgive the Nazis not because they deserve it but because I deserve it.'
> Concentration camp survivor, Eva Kor

If I backpedal a smidge, I'm not arguing that really bad stuff is anything other than really bad stuff. But if we lower the bar from 'really bad stuff' to everyday fuck-ups that befall us all – just because you've messed up doesn't mean you are messed up. Or, to bastardize a phrase that I heard on the radio, it hurts to let go but sometimes it's even more painful to hang on.

> 'Here I am,
> peppered with the shrapnel of old.
> Scars from a thousand bastards,
> that no make up could ever cover.'
> From Therapy, by Aron Kirk

This is top-shelf stuff so, to give it some credibility, let's defer to Immanuel Kant, undoubtedly a clever bloke and a big cheese in the world of philosophy. His 800-pager, *A Critique of Pure Reason*, written in eighteenth-century German, didn't win any awards. Probably because he spent a large part of it pontificating on the calculation $5 + 7 = 12$, suggesting there is nothing in the numbers 5 and 7 by which the number 12 can be inferred.

Why Mr Kant, why? This head-scratching befuddlement aside, his reflections on cause and effect opened up a crack of enlightenment just large enough for some light to shine through.

He'll be turning in his grave at my summary of his ideas (sorry big man) but using some of *his* words it boils down to this – our experience of things is always of the phenomenal world as conveyed by our senses: we do not have direct access to things in themselves, the so-called noumenal world.

Using *my* words, our senses don't transmit the world to us but, rather, we use them to knit a version of reality that's a combination of sensory data with what we already think, know, feel, and want to believe. We use this combination of sensory information and pre-existing experience to construct our perception of reality.

Having softened you up, I'm with Mr Kant in suggesting reality isn't actually real. Mr Einstein also agreed, by the way, suggesting that 'reality is merely an illusion, albeit a very persistent one'.

But oh my gosh, it sure feels real. This life I'm living, these experiences I'm experiencing, these feelings coursing through my awareness, this laptop I'm tapping away on … are you saying these are just special effects?

Reality is uber-convincing. We feel as though we're sitting in our bodies, viewing the world through the clear glass windows of our eyes and hearing birdsong via our perfectly formed ears. We think we're experiencing the world as it truly is. But we're actually not.

195

Cutting to the chase, your brain doesn't see, hear, or feel anything. It can't, locked away as it is in a dark chamber, aka your skull. It relies on your senses detecting stimuli

> 'Who are you gonna believe, me or your own eyes?'
>
> Groucho Marx

in the outside world that it then translates into an experience. Your brain is foraging for information to weave into your memory and perception to create a view of the world whose detail is so compelling that we never question it. Dan Gilbert's analogy is to imagine you are a counterfeiter, producing £20 notes. You are also acting as the victim. You are the producer of fake £20 notes and passing them off to yourself, without even holding them up to the light.

What we're experiencing is always us doing something to ourselves. It can only ever be that. It's a thought, brought to life by your consciousness, which creates a feeling. In *this* moment. The feeling exists now, even though the experience might have happened 15 years ago. It's the perfect system; consciousness grabs the thought and seduces you into believing it to be real.

No matter how scary or traumatic your experience of life may be, the idea is to realize that it's only your own thinking that you're experiencing and, with that realization, that self-same 'thinking' should lose much of its hold on you. You may still experience horrible feelings but, once you realize that they're caused by what's inside you, you don't feel compelled to change the world in order to feel good.

You have to change you. Which to be brutally honest, can feel a lot more difficult than trying to change the world.

But here's where it gets really interesting. If your thinking is killing you, in some cases literally, then surely the reverse must also be true: your thinking can cure you and save you.

Let's duct-tape science and insight together for a big bang moment of what I'm right this minute trademarking as 'sc-insight'™. Recalling the 2%ers diagram from earlier (I know you've forgotten it so I've stuck it in again cos I love you), everyone has an upper and lower level of well-being.

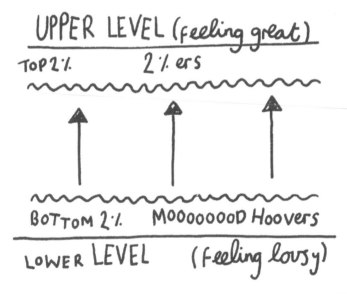

UPPER LEVEL (feeling great)

TOP 2%   2% ers

BOTTOM 2%   MOoooooooD Hoovers

LOWER LEVEL   (feeling lousy)

I've spent 12 years seeking out happy people and following them around, stalking them, in an attempt to find their secrets.

The 2%ers, those who are stand-out happy and full of energy, what do you think they're *thinking?* When the Monday morning alarm goes, what's running through their heads?

In case the penny hasn't dropped, their thoughts are much more likely to be positive, upbeat, optimistic, and anticipatory of the day bringing something good.

Remember, you are *feeling* your thinking. Hence the 2%ers are registering at the upper levels of the happiness Richter scale. Their upbeat thoughts create feelings of engagement (in my PhD data, they scored significantly higher on feelings of joy, enthusiasm, excitement, and inspiration)

Now imagine the rest of the population – ordinary people, going about their life on autopilot. The alarm goes off at stupid o'clock on a wet Monday; what are they thinking? More crucially, what have they *learned* to think about a wet Monday morning?

Hence what are they *feeling?* My data shows they are registering higher on stress, despondency, anxiety, and depression.

I don't think I can say it any simpler than that. I can make it more complicated by sharing more PhD thesis with you, but why would I? Remember, my research has been about 'intentional strategies' that 2%ers do. By that, I mean learned behaviours, habits, ways of thinking … life hacks, cheat codes … call them whatever you want, it boils down to attitudinal choices.

Thinking.

Get that bit right and feelings will follow.

The Big Swim

Ladies and gents, let me illustrate via the true story of Slovakian, Martin Strel, a guy who swam the Amazon. For younger readers, the Amazon is a very long river named after an online book shop.

Some stats and facts for you. Martin swam 2300 miles in 66 days. At the end his blood pressure was at heart-attack levels and his entire body was wriggling with larvae that had buried under his skin. Larvae aside, the main dangers were pirates, piranhas, snakes, bull sharks, and crocs (the animal, not the fashion faux pas). Indeed, his team had buckets of blood that they threw into the river to distract the piranhas. Add deadly diseases (malaria, dengue fever, dysentery); floating debris (he was hit head on by a floating VW camper van); and the fact that if you pee in the water it attracts a very dangerous fish called the candirú, which lodges up human orifices with a razor-like spike and then sucks your blood.

Martin has also swum the Nile, so he's a proper bona fide nutter. I'm not expecting you to do likewise. However, for the

199

purposes of this analogy I want you to *imagine* that you're swimming the Amazon. Swimming cap and crocodile repellent on, I'm putting you into the mouth of the river and setting you the challenge of swimming upstream. I'm coming with you in my guise as 'Analogy Man' with my pithy catchphrase: 'comparing one thing with another, typically for the purpose of explanation or clarification'. I'll be your support crew, in the boat, manning the buckets of blood.

We're seeking the source of the Amazon. This is not your local swimming baths so rather than a dozen 'no petting' type rules there's just one; for your own sake, no peeing. *Absolutely* no peeing. Analogy Man will support you all the way but if that candirú finds its way in, I'm not sucking it out!

This is what you'll notice. The mouth of the Amazon is a muddy meandering mess, a vast delta of brownness infested with flotsam and jetsam from way upstream. You'll be bumped and bruised by big items. Expect shopping trolleys, fridges, cars, and whole trees.

But if you keep front-crawling upstream the river begins to narrow. There are fewer abandoned shopping trolleys. A thousand miles into your journey and you'll be swimming in clean water, the Amazon cutting a channel through dense Brazilian rainforest. It's rather beautiful. There might be a few fallen branches floating by but no VWs or fridges. Two thousand miles upstream and the Amazon has narrowed considerably. You're actually in Peru, near the source. The river is fast and crystal clear. No mud. No crocs. No debris.

You can pee freely because there are no candirú this far upstream.

Keep swimming and eventually the river disappears and you investigate the rock it spouts from. It's fresh, clean, drinkable water, the purest possible. The entire 2300-mile muddy mess started out right here.

And Analogy Man would leap into action, pulling his pants a little too high in excited anticipation.

Wedgie Man perhaps?

We all have access to the clear and un-muddied source of thinking. Jamie Smart calls it clarity. He's bang on. This purity is where we start out but as time goes by we learn certain habits, we experience certain experiences, we learn to be defensive, fault-finding, pessimistic, and negative. Our purity of thought becomes a muddy mess. Those bastard candirú fish are Metaphor Man's best ally, infecting you with razor-like barbs of self-criticism and self-doubt. My goodness, once they're lodged in, they're very difficult to get out!

That VW campervan of a thought, the one that knocks you sideways, that's drifted from upstream. It's a thought from your past. Those bitey, stingy, sharp-toothed piranha thoughts, they're your memories of injustices and wrongdoings from bygone days.

Those dangers lurking in the stream of your consciousness – who put them there? Where did they come from?

It's rather painful to realize that *you* put those thoughts into the river of consciousness.

But if you can get back to the source, the un-muddied crystal-clear stream from which thought emerges, you have a fresh start. You can add nice memories, fabulous relationships, kind deeds, moments of joy, pride in your achievements. If you stick these into your stream of consciousness you'll run into them downstream but instead of being battered you'll be feeling totally alive, refreshed in positivity of thought that gives energy of body.

It's worth waking up to the awareness that you have a choice of thoughts and, secondly, that you can learn to direct your attention towards good, clean, healthy ones. The essence is that thoughts are streaming by and whichever you choose to focus on becomes your reality. So, at one level, it makes good sense to wait for a good one. But applying some effort to generating some nice thoughts and learning to give them a positive spin surely means that your river of consciousness will contain many more resourceful thoughts.

In the Amazon analogy, inside-out thinking is about sourcing purity of thought. If you were able to access a higher level of consciousness and realize that everything was created from thought, you wouldn't have to fish the crocs, piranhas, candirú, and VWs out – they simply wouldn't be in there because, guess what, it's you who put them in there in the first place.

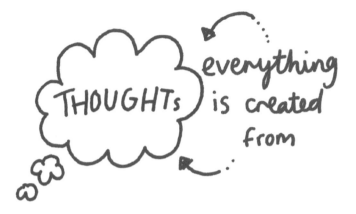

One other thing worth noting about consciousness is its neutrality. Its job is not to question why you've hopped aboard a particular thought. Consciousness just does its thing, turning your chosen thought into a feeling which you experience as living, breathing, full-colour reality.

Remember, you have a million thoughts buffering, waiting in a queue, hoping to be the chosen one. Imagine, for argument's sake, you jump aboard a thought about your ex-husband. He's 'ex' for a reason so, once aboard that thought, your consciousness digs up all the old stories and hey presto, your moment is filled with loathing and hatred. Once you're on that thought, it's easy to jump onto the next one floating by: his infidelities. And then there are some dark thoughts about your ex-mother-in-law, she was a hag, and you're plunged into a really bad 20 minutes.

To add emotional insult to your mental injury, you're been feeling bad NOW about something that happened 10 years ago.

If you're not careful your whole life plays out like this. These 20 minutes soon add up! You live a counterfeit existence without ever realizing you're the counterfeiter.

One Moment Please

Before we finish, I need a quick moment about moments. I need to explain why I put the previous 'NOW' in capitals. Why did I make it all shouty?

The whole 'inner peace' shebang has an Eastern lineage. The hippy movement created a crack in the pervading Western culture that was just large enough to let some ancient Eastern wisdom squeeze through.

This counterculture became a movement. Spirituality gained traction via The Beatles' White Album. George Harrison played a sitar. Skinny Indians, chubby Buddhists, flowers in your hair, a sexual revolution, free love, *man*. The movement reached maximum flower power when an Indian Swami opened Woodstock in 1969.

The Hippy Code reads thus: 'Do your own thing, wherever you have to do it and whenever you want. Drop out. Leave society as you have known it. Leave it utterly. Blow the mind of every straight person you can reach. Turn them on, if not to drugs, then to beauty, love, honesty, fun.'[1]

I'll inhale to that.

---

[1] Interestingly, by 'straight', they meant your standard 9–5, middle-class, rat-race person.

J. Krishnamurti, the great Indian philosopher, travelled the world for 50 years on a global speaking tour. As a spiritual teacher I guess his gig strapline was something like 'attempting to convey through words that which is beyond words'. I'm imagining it was a lot quieter than a Stones tour.

Towards the end of his 50-year marathon tenure, he surprised his audience by asking, 'Do you want to know my secret?' His followers leaned in. Many had been following him for five decades and not quite grasped his meaning.

'This is my secret,' he said. 'I don't mind what happens.'

Once again, I wasn't there but I'm imagining a collective audience eyeroll, 'WTF? Is that it? After 50 years?'

This is black belt happiness ninja level because when you reach the point of 'I don't mind what happens' it implies that internally I am in alignment with whatever *does* happen. It points, once again, to the fact that everything is neutral until you apply thinking to it.

Buddhists have a phrase, tathātā, which is best translated as 'suchness' or the 'as-is-ness' of the moment. I love that phrase; *as-is-ness*. It's so simple yet takes you to near-altitude-sickness levels of personal development.

In order to create reality we have to perceive everything as something. We label things to give them meaning, whereas tathātā just lets it be what it is. That Hollywood mystic, Doris Day, she was in the right ballpark with her 'que será será' mantra. When she invented the original footballing chant, 'Whatever will be will be, we going to Wem-ber-lee', she was tathātā-ing.

Enlightenment comes when you twig that the 'suchness of life' is, of course, no more than the *as-is-ness* of this moment. Opposition toward the moment is one of the main features of your human operating system. Your ego's a hungry bastard. It doesn't want *this* moment, it wants a better one, in the future, so it's mad keen for you to get this moment out of the way. It makes you impatient with this 'now' without realizing that this particular now is all it ever has (that's because when it gets to the next now, that also becomes 'this now', hence your ego is in a never-ending chase for a better moment).

We're back to tathātā and Doris Day's que será será. *This* moment – the only moment there ever is – is accepted and welcomed. It's probably the ultimate freedom. I say 'probably' because it's something I'm able to do intermittently but is beyond my spiritual pay grade to be able to do consistently.

It boils down to whether you want to make the present moment your friend or your enemy. Remembering that the present moment is inseparable from life – 'now' is all you ever have – so you're really deciding what kind of a relationship you want to have with life. Once you have decided you want the present moment to be your friend, it is up to you to make the first move. You can't sit there, all sulky, waiting for life to offer an olive branch. Become friendly toward it, welcome it no matter what disguise it's wearing, and soon you will see the results. Life becomes friendly toward you; people become helpful, circumstances cooperative.

Inside-out, innate thinking, 3 Ps, serendipity, karma, mindfulness, the law of attraction, spirituality ... I don't care what you call it.

> 'I always admired atheists. I think it takes a lot of faith.'
>
> *Diane Frolov*

Befriending the present moment is befriending life itself.

For me, the best way to befriend the present moment is to be grateful. Gratitude is like fertilizer for happiness.

As a devout non-religious person (I describe myself as 'not for prophet') I can't help developing a sneaky admiration for Buddhism. Firstly because it's the only religion that doesn't have a God and secondly, because it's the one that's most closely aligned to the science of well-being.

~~fertilizer~~ gratitude

Here's how clever Buddhism is – to paraphrase Thích Nhất Hạnh (a Vietnamese monk), most people would consider walking on water a miracle. But the real miracle is not to walk on water, but to walk on earth.

That's insanely sage. Every day we are engaged in a miracle which we don't even recognize: blue sky, white clouds,

207

green leaves, fresh air, smiling children, warm Cornish pasties …

Sadly, my eloquence lets me down.

Julie Andrews sang about bright copper kettles, raindrops on roses, whiskers on schnitzel and kittens with noodles (yum!). There was other stuff in there, and she probably reeled them off in a different order but she was in the right happiness ballpark. Louis Armstrong too; he was seeing skies of blue and clouds of white, bright blessed day and dark sacred night. He saw friends shaking hands saying how do you do when really they were saying 'I love you'.

All is a miracle. If you begin from there, anything else is a bonus.

Julie, you're bang on. Focus your attention on your favourite things. And Louis, I'm with you mate, what an utterly wonderful world.

Past and Future Tense

Let's revise ego one last time, cos I know you've forgotten; it's who you think you are, the voice inside your head that gives you a running commentary. You are the central character in the plot of your life and for your ego to exist, it needs things to happen to you. It needs friends, enemies, traumas, love … your ego needs events to unfold because these outside influences are your story.

If your ego's like mine, it loves a clock. Time is ticking. Life's hectic, a bit of a rush. There's too much to do and not enough time to do it.

The story of your day is 'headless chicken'. Almost always!

> 'The reasonable man adapts himself to the world; the unreasonable one persists in trying to adapt the world to himself. Therefore all progress depends on the unreasonable man.'
>
> *George Bernard Shaw*

Have you ever noticed that nearly every thought you think is concerned with the past or future? That's because your sense of self depends on the past for your identity and on the future for its fulfilment.

I've just twigged why, in the English language, you can have a past and future tense. Because that's exactly what they create – tension!

> 'If you look back in anger, you may walk into a lamppost. If you look forward with hope, you may be coshed from behind.'
>
> *A no-win scenario from the redoubtable Philip Ardagh*

To the ego, the present moment is, at best, only useful as a means to an end. It gets you to some future moment that is considered more important. In other words, you are never fully 'here' because you are always busy trying to get somewhere else.

I was trapped in this world for several decades, a bad case of irritable bastard syndrome in which the present moment was treated as if it were an obstacle to be overcome. This is where impatience, frustration, and stress morph into everyday reality. They become your normal state. Life (which is always now) is seen as a 'problem', something to be rushed through, an annoyance, and you come to inhabit a world of problems that all need to be solved before you can be happy, fulfilled, or really start living.

At surface level, the present moment is 'what's happening to you'. Since what happens changes continuously, it seems that every day of your life consists of thousands of moments in which different things are happening. Time is seen as the endless succession of moments, some 'good' some 'bad'. Yet, if you take Poirot's magnifying glass and have a good close-up examination of your moments, you'll discover the bizarre paradox – there aren't as many as you think.

In fact, there's just the one.

This fucking one!

Life is always now. Your entire life unfolds in this constancy of *this present moment*.

I'm not talking about doing away with clock time. That'd be bordering on silly. You'd keep missing your train. I'm talking of psychological time, the time in your head, the ego's endless preoccupation with past and future and its unwillingness to be aligned with the only time that's real.

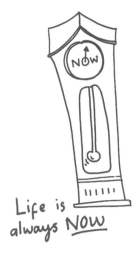

Life is always NOW

For the ego to survive, it must make past and future time more important than the present moment.

But hang on, there's a past, right? I have a past? I can remember it! I've got a chuffing newspaper to prove it was there. I've got a bin full of yesterday's rubbish and a laptop full of holiday snaps.

Well, yes, kind of. Your past was a 'present moment' that doesn't exist anywhere, except in your mind. It's not stored. Any memory of what happened yesterday (or before) is nothing more than you recalling it NOW. The same for imagining what might happen tomorrow. In an OMG blinding flash of obviousness, tomorrow, when it arrives in your life, is yet another 'present moment'.

It's not Groundhog Day, it's Groundhog Moment. Hence (quantum physicist) David Bohm's conclusion that, 'ultimately, all moments are really one. Therefore now is eternity.'

211

Yeah, that!

People have written about this stuff for thousands of years, but they're normally mystics, scholars, philosophers, theologians, muftis, or maverick scientists. And, hand on heart, none of them has made it very clear. At least, not clear enough for me to properly grasp. So, on the one hand, if the sages have failed to provide clarity, there's a decent argument to say my wife is right – the last thing you need is for a bloke from Derby to wade in!

But on the other hand, what if these big-ticket items have always been tackled by the wrong people? Quantum physicists, the enlightened, those sitting next to God … they've all had a go at explaining what I'm about to have a go at, and failed.

Because they're too clever!

They've written tomes. *A Course in Miracles*, billed as 'the classic guide to modern spirituality', runs to 300,000 impenetrable words. Eisberg's classic book *Quantum Physics*, which includes chapters on crystallography, Fourier Integral Description of a Wave Group, and Time–Independent Perturbation Theory, comes in at 260,000 words (and is currently £220 on Amazon).

There's got to be a gap in the market for an average bloke from Middle England to sum it up in 300 words.

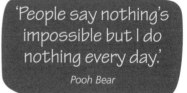

'People say nothing's impossible but I do nothing every day.'

Pooh Bear

Plus, I like a challenge!

To summarize the last 4000 years of personal development, your Doctor of Happiness and part-time children's author reckons it's something like this: you are not watching the movie of your life – you are writing, directing, and projecting it.

First base, we're not dealing with what we think. We're dealing with the fact *that* we think. Each one of us exists in a thought-created experience, and therefore, we are only ever one thought away from a whole new 'reality'. It takes some getting your head around, the fact that life is not happening to you, it's happening *within* you.

Second base, you are not feeling the outside world, you are feeling (and therefore living) your thinking. That's a bastard of a sentence because it's a complete reversal of how it seems. You'll swear blind that your teenager's anxiety is coming from being bullied on social media, or that your partner's rage is caused by her workplace making her re-apply for her own job, or your irritability is caused by a neighbour who continues to play loud music. Or, indeed, that my daughter's feelings are coming from a piece of pink cloth that she called Pinky.

Third base, your entire life is lived in the present moment. So more tathātā-ing and less stressing. The world isn't going to bend and mould itself to fit your exact requirements. The world is going to continue to do its thing. Learning to be best pals with the present moment is a much bigger deal than it sounds.

And finally, positive psychology provides some solutions. This new branch of learning has started to examine the lives of those who are already feeling great. The science of what's

213

going well is a significant breakthrough because rather than inventing cures, we're studying the people who already have them. Yes, there's a bit of effort involved but it's perfectly possible to re-train your thinking, swinging it away from its default negativity bias of when the dog bites and the bee stings, towards cream-coloured ponies and crisp apple strudels. If you are the creator of your thoughts, you may as well get busy sourcing some crackers.

My advice is to read this section again. And maybe again after that.

It's philosophy, psychology, science, and spirituality blended in a NutriBullet. It might be difficult to swallow but it's nourishing.

It also happens to be the truth as I currently understand it.

Now, go do whatever you want with it.

Part 5

YOGI, BOO-BOO, AND THE HOMOS

215

The Hitchhiker's Guide to the Galaxy got away with being a trilogy in four parts. I have a little bit of unfinished business so I thought I'd stretch it to five…

> Sponsored by the word **Kōan** (公案). Japanese / n. / ˈkəʊ.ɑn / koh-an. Lit. public record, or official business; principles of reality existing outside of subjective opinion; an 'unanswerable' question or riddle, used in Zen to facilitate awakening.

The Worm that Turned

Steven Johnson apparently said this: 'We take the ideas we've inherited or that we've stumbled across, and we jigger them into some new shape.'[1]

That's exactly what I've done, jiggered – reshaped my previous work, tidied it up, clarified a few bits, and inched it forward. It might not look like it but, truth be told, I've worked ever so hard.

And here you are, almost at the end of the book. I'm nervous. What do you think of it? Should I have toned it down, or up? And Part 4, that inside-out 'reality isn't real' stuff, the bit my wife warned me *not* to include ('People don't need to know this shit Andy') which I went and included anyway.

---

[1] S. Johnson (2011) Where Good Ideas Come From: The Seven Patterns of Innovation. *New York: Penguin.*

Yogi Berra (the man, not Boo-Boo's sidekick) is classic quotable fodder, a man so silly that his sayings loop back on themselves to somehow make perfect sense. 'I'm not going to buy my kids an encyclopaedia. Let them walk to school like I did', is pretty good. 'You can observe a lot by just watching' is even better. You have to think about 'No one goes there nowadays, it's too crowded' before its sublime idiocy hits you.

So it won't surprise you that he also said, 'When you come to a fork in the road, take it.'

That's genius, right there.

Life's path is, of course, a multi-pronged fork. To follow the crowd, take the fork onto the big wide multi-lane tarmacked highway. It's well signposted. The M25 of life – it's perfectly fine, if a little crowded.

Go for it!

Some of the other forks are a little less travelled. In fact some of the least worn paths are a bit jungley. You might need a cutlass to chop through the undergrowth but, as you do so, you make the path easier for fellow travellers. Look, I'm not up my arse enough to claim that I'm the first along the jungle route. There are a few muddy footprints and evidence of chopping. But while the double-decker bus route continues to drive life's tourists along the tarmacked superhighway, I'm with Helen Keller; life's either a daring adventure or nothing at all.

Unfortunately, Helen couldn't see the view so let me explain – it's *amaaaaaazing!*

You'll need a packed lunch, an energy drink, and lots of faith. Not faith in me, faith in the belief that by reading this book, particularly Part 4, you're walking the trail, marking the way, helping others to get to a much better place.

Not, by the way, that there's anything overtly wrong with the well-worn double-decker route. Most people travel this route. It's perfectly fine. Certainly easier. It's the obvious route. But look around at your fellow commuters and ask yourself, do you want to end up like them? All that time sitting watching the world go by? Might it not be better to deviate?

I started with the brevity of life, so I'll finish with it. I'm a firm believer that the best way to prepare for death is to live an epic life so my final two final messages are about worms and evolution.

Worms first.

Darwin's final book, published in 1881, was an epic tome about the humble life of the earthworm.[2] No plot spoilers

[2] C. Darwin (1881) The Formation of Vegetable Mould through the Action of Worms. *London: John Murray.*

from me but basically his argument is that worms have superpowers. Ten tons of earth passes through the body of your average worm and collectively, they have tilled the soil and changed the face of the earth.

Your life is a game. Since the day you were born you've been playing dodge the earthworm.

Dodge the earthworm

But nobody can dodge them forever. They're relentless. The worms are a-coming. One day, they'll devour you. You'll be passed through the body of an earthworm. Perfectly recycled. Part of the tilling process.

For those left behind you'll just be a photo, a few YouTube snippets, and a memory.

So a decent bit of advice is 'do your best to be a good one'.

And finally, your genetic hand-me-down.

Remember, your brain was in full bloom at two. You peaked early, before you could control your bowels.

At 14, you *thought* you knew everything. Much more than your parents, for sure. You actually knew diddly squat.

At 30, you did know some stuff.

At 50, you know a lot of stuff.

At 90, you know everything but you can't remember any of it. Not even who you are. And your bowels have learned to be two again.

Beyond all these ages is wisdom, the penny dropper when you realize that no matter how much you learn, you actually know next to nothing. And cutting through them all is something that has nothing to do with age: insight.

Famously, Archimedes had his insight in the bath, and Morten Harket had his in a recording studio. Your 'AHA' moment doesn't have to come as a blinding crash, bang, wallop flash of enlightenment. It can *drip drip drip drip drip drip* its way into your life like inside-out thinking has done with me.

In previous books I've analogized about a swimming lesson. I've walked my readers through the footbath of academia, splashed around in the shallow end, and eventually made it to the deep end. I've done the hand-holding as we progress.

This last section is different. In summary, this is it: all we are is peace, love, and wisdom, and the power to create the illusion that we're not.

And straight away, we're in the deep end. Flailing probably!

Revisiting thought and consciousness one last time. If you have 80,000 thoughts a day, that's 2.5 billion in your lifetime. Each thought is brought to life by your inner special effects team that is 'Consciousness FX'.

221

The life of each thought is only as long as you think it.

You can't have racism if you know that everything is made of thought. Racism isn't an actual 'thing'. It's a thought that someone treats as though it's true. Babies aren't racist because they haven't learned to be. Yet! No one has taught them the ridiculous thought that skin colour implies anything other than different pigment, just like different hair colour.

In the same way, you're not born into a political party. You're not born left or right wing, you learn these leanings according to the messages you absorb. Indeed, other people's thinking seeps into yours.

We've drawn lines around territories and states and countries. Your garden fence or line of conifers, they define what's yours. We belong. It gives us an identity, an ego, a script, a clan to belong to, and another gang of people over the other side of the line that we can hate.

Religion. Same.

Everything.

Same.

The Rise of the Homo

Homo sapiens is Latin for 'wise man'. *Who knew?*

When faced with a radical crisis to the point where survival is threatened by seemingly insurmountable problems, a species will either become extinct or go through an evolutionary leap. It's similar to the analogy of painting your egg or hatching.

Zip back to pre-mammal times and you'd find the oceans awash with life. Science is not 100% clear but the consensus is that there was no life out of the water. At some point one of the fish had to go first, let's call her Sandra, flapping her fins onto a rock, eyeballing the volcanoes and forests through her glassy fishy eyes, feeling the gravitational pressures, and flipping back into the ocean where life was more buoyant and a whole lot easier.

Sandra tried again and again and again, and much later her eggs and grand-eggs would adapt to life on land, grow feet instead of fins, develop lungs instead of gills. It seems unlikely that Sandra would venture into such an alien environment and undergo an evolutionary transformation unless she really had to. She didn't jump, she was pushed.

The point is one of evolutionary adaptation caused by crisis. Sandra's sea must have been getting too salty or drying up. Now I'm not saying we've reached that point quite yet, but with depleted forests and an occasional drop of water being discovered in our plastic oceans, we're maybe heading that way.

Chill. The apocalypse might be coming but I'm not suggesting it's going to happen tomorrow, next week, or in your lifetime.

In terms of human population it's fair to say that it took us a while to get going. In the tenth century the world population was approximately 4 million – that's half the total

223

THE LITTLE BOOK OF BEING BRILLIANT

of modern-day London. Reminder, that was the *global* population. Mother nature had an ingenious way of keeping us in check. Just as we thought we'd nailed it with mass copulation causing rising population, she'd send a Malthusian drought, flood, shipload of bubonic plague, or bout of Spanish flu to show us who's boss.

Thinned out, we'd start copulating again. But we're a canny species. We built desalination plants and flood defences. Then Alexander Fleming left something in a petri dish overnight and, boom, antibiotics were born. Then, more recently someone invented Lemsip, and man flu, although still terribly dangerous, lost its culling edge.

Think about it for a second. For you to exist you have to come from an unbroken line of evolution in which every generation survived long enough to reach maturity and pass on their genes. You and Sandra are related. You are the cutting edge of evolution, the point of the arrow, the best that homo sapiens currently has to offer.

There's a rather big question lurking; something along the lines of 'It took all of eternity so far to produce you. Are you worth it?'

With three hundred words to go, that's too big to elaborate, other than to give a resounding YES!

Close your eyes and imagine the best possible version of you because that's who you really are! You have powers beyond superhero status.

'You are one in over 7.4 billion humans on this planet and although you might not be able to change the whole world, you can make a few of those worlds a tiny bit brighter.'

Emily Coxhead

You can play a huge part in saving the planet.

Here's how …

There's a huge difference being well-being and being well off. There are currently 7.5 billion of us, mostly crammed into cities, cheek by jowl, consuming the planet at an alarming rate.

The only way to consume less is to be happy with consuming less and the only way to get happy with consuming less is to understand that your happiness doesn't come from consumption.

I've worked hard to realign your thinking, to stop chasing more, to realize that when you're content, you have enough.

If you grasp the themes of this book and apply them to your life, you will be content. Hence, you live from a bedrock of gratitude and appreciation. The chasing stops. The histrionics become history. Relationships blossom. The present moment becomes your best buddy.

Evolution doesn't have to work in a straight line. Maybe we've accidentally backwardly evolved from Homo sapiens ('wise man') into a less wise 'Homo consumption' or 'Homo narcissistic'?

We need to boldly go where no homo has gone before.

What if our next incarnation is 'Homo conscious', 'Homo nowuss', 'Homo contentedness' or, dare I venture, 'Homo happiuss'?

If, in 5 million years, our skulls are dug up and examined we many find there are signs of transition towards a new type of human – an altogether more community-centric one. A homo with fewer shoes, less tech, and where people stopped watching *Love Island* and started to create communities where love, relationships, and the people were real.

Our forebears will look back at these early changes in skull shape and recognize that Homo sapiens had been mid-transition.

In the year 5,002,020 they might look around at their green, lush, fully-stocked planet; their plastic-free oceans; their happy and content communities and thank their lucky stars that they're descended from us; the new breed of happy humans.

What if we are the missing link?

Let's make it happen!

Acknowledgements

A big shout out to:

All the people whose work I've leaned on over the years. David (Naked Leader) Taylor and Paul (SUMO) McGee always make it into my books. Guys, if only you knew the impact your books had on me. Thank you.

Big-ups to Jamie Smart whose impact has been huge. Some of the concepts in Part 4 were borrowed from his books and podcasts. There are a lot of 3 Ps gurus who tie me up in knots. Jamie, thanks for unravelling me.

Darren Beniston. Daz, what can I say? Mate, you make me laugh and cry. Thank you.

And, gosh, who thought I'd ever be thanking Russell Brand? Brilliant books fella. The podcast is epic too. Advice (not that your stellar career needs it) but please do more ranting on your poddy. Use those big words and long sentences that we can't understand. You're far more entertaining than your guests ever are.

Family. Yes you lot! I'm such a lucky man.

And finally, a thank you to my mates. The lads I used to go to school with and now, 40 years later, I go out on a Thursday night with. They don't actually give a flying fuck about my books and that's great. They haven't read any of them. They never ask about them. They won't ever read this thank you. That's why Thursday night is, and will always be, ego-less.

About the Author

Dr Andy Cope is a qualified teacher, trainer, author, happiness expert and learning junkie. At the time of writing he is the UK's one and only Doctor of Happiness (yes, he knows it's cheesy but he reckons it's more socially acceptable than the alternative 'Dr Feelgood').

Andy has written a host of best-selling books on the subjects of positive psychology, leadership, and emotional intelligence. He is also a prolific children's author. His *Spy Dog* series has been a global best seller and he's recently written *Diary of a Brilliant Kid* and *A Teenager's Guide to Life* in an attempt to bring the lessons of mental wealth to a younger audience.

He works with an amazing bunch of talented trainers who deliver workshops and keynotes across the world. And while the trainers are fab, it's behind the scenes where the magic happens. Thanks to M, Jen, Lou, Karina, Chewy, and Ames.

Andy is married to Louise and they have two grown-up kiddywinks, Scrump and Bwana (everyone has stupid nicknames in our house, even Bubba the cat whose real name is Eva. I think?)

Check his work out at www.artofbrilliance.co.uk and his school well-being website at www.brilliant.school.

Andy can be contacted at andy@artofbrilliance.co.uk